A Collection of Voices

the dawn of global awareness

as expressed in the letters to Earth Day 1990.

PK Publishing, Palo Alto

Thank you

Len Erickson, Laura Harris, Michael Winkler, Kellogg John Hooker, Jack
Russo
Paul Sposato, Leslie Gordon, Peter Whidden, Don Beeson
&
Members of Bay Area Action (BAA)
for your help on this book.

Library of Congress Cataloging in Publication Data:
Wright, Peter Hoe
Wright, Peter, ed. 1943 -
     A Collection of Voices
     the dawn of global awareness as expressed in the letters to Earth Day 1990
     Palo Alto, California, USA
     200 pages

PK Publishing, 1420 College Avenue, Palo Alto, California, USA
Cover by: Robert Steven Pawlak, San Francisco, California, USA
Printed by: Malloy Lithographing, Inc., 5411 Jackson Rd., Ann Arbor, MI, USA

Library of Congress Catalog Card Number: 91-90190
ISBN   0-944271-10-3

Dedicated to:

Min Thein

Contents:

Preface   i

Introduction   ii

1. Suited to the Task?   1
2. From Everywhere; From Everyone   17
3. But Why the Trees?   33
4. There is no Sanctuary   47
5. How Many?   61
6. Econology   73
7. . . . for the People?   89
8. Stewardship   101
9. Ceremonies and Celebrations   113
10. Poems, Pledges, and Songs   131
11. . . . and the Young Shall Inherit . . . ?   147
12. *To a new consciousness awakening!*   161

Postscript   179

Addendum:
    "The Isthmus of Karelia" by Serge Tsvetkov   182
    "The Integrity of Creation" by Sister Betty Wolcott   184

Preface

Earth Day 1990 dwarfed all previous political events. More than 200 million people were brought together in 141 countries. In Manhattan alone, the 1990 Earth Day was more than twice as large as Woodstock had been two decades earlier.

The international headquarters took full advantage of modern communications technology. We employed computer networks, express delivery services, fax machines, telexes, and huge banks of telephones. But the vast majority of messages we sent and received were plain, old-fashioned letters.

Most of the correspondence was routine: requests from teachers for environmental curricular material; requests for speakers and celebrities; requests for advice about crowd control, insurance, and emergency medical facilities; requests for general information about recycling, rainforest destruction, global warming, solar energy, toxic waste, vanishing species, human population growth, ozone depletion, etc.

To handle the sheer volume, we were forced to create bureaucratic systems. A request for information about global warming automatically elicited fact sheet number 4. We lacked the time and resources to respond personally to each of the tens of thousands of letters flooding in.

Peter Wright, who bestrode this river of incoming mail and channelled it into the proper floodgates, found some of the letters deeply moving. He could not respond thoughtfully to them in the heat of the campaign. So he put aside letters that he felt were "special", with the intention of editing them into a book someday after life quieted down.

Life quieted down, and this is Peter's book. The letters were not chosen for political consistency or scientific rigor or balance. These are simply the letters that Peter found most touching or intriguing. Yet, these unheralded grass roots correspondents--united only by their deep concern for the fate of the planet--may provide authentic insight into the soul of this emerging movement.

Denis Hayes
Chairman, Earth Day 1990

Introduction

How large a hole must there be in the ozone before the blue-haired old lady living in Florida stops using aerosol? How many tons of smoke must rise above the Amazon before our local supermarket stops buying canned Brazilian beef? How much farmland must lose its productivity? How many vegetables must lose their wholesomeness? How many farm workers their health? Where is the line in the sand at which all the horrors finally overwhelm our adaptability, and in our desperation, in our frustration with the promises of politicians and the accidents of corporations, we grab the last sword left us and with it pen that long-thought-of-but-not-yet-written letter from our frightened heart to an anonymous savior some-where whose reply, we hope, we pray, like a kiss, will make it all better?

Perhaps it was with just such unconscious thoughts that 80,000 people wrote letters to Earth Day. One letter received represents many others which, for some reason, were never written, or not sent, or only thought out and then discarded as hopeless into the waste-bins of resigned and tired minds. Still, 80,000 letters did arrive, representing millions of people of like mind, all pointing towards one moment as a day of hope when the kiss of that celebration would (at least temporarily) soothe the hurt. I read as many as 70,000 of those letters. During the two and one half months I was with Earth Day, the shared sentiments of millions of individuals passed before my eyes. Their emotions could not be kept from becoming part of me. I do not blush to say that the sum of their concerns and feelings affected me . . . that at times I wept. In my search for an answer to the ecological predicament we are in, finally I sensed that in these letters lay an answer.

As I peeled off the layers, I tossed the common requests for information into the boxes guaranteeing them the right response and handling. From the fast moving stream, I pulled and set aside the interesting letters, not always having time to read them right then. They were easy to spot; they began differently: "At 78, having for many years been an advocate of Natural Living . . ." or, "I am a prisoner and want the children of the world to know what it is like to play in a stream of clear water," or even (from a 14 year old) "Help! I am going to die if I don't get an Earth Day T-shirt."

The letters are now bound and printed on the boiled-down stuff of trees. Divided into twelve chapters--progressing from the simple problems of the 1970's to the complex problems and spiritual awakening of the 1990's--

they continue the story of our species' struggles to make life better. Through all the letters, Earth Day seemed to represent an ideal. The authors, in writing to that ideal, called upon their better selves and gave their concerns heightened expression. Even the tens of thousands which were passed over often had a captivating quality:

My name is Amanda Boggs and I live in West Virginia. Not many non-West Virginians are aware of this fact, but there is a huge problem, namely in Braxton County, of landfills. It astounds me that people want to use our precious land to fill with trash.

I know there are thousands of problems of more concern all around the world, too many to even think of, but I really didn't realize the magnitude of our (and our Earth's) state until something occurred that concerned my local environment. I wish to help . . .

Some letters were doubtful of Earth Day's purpose; some were even hostile. An official of one international Christian organization wondered whether her church should support us since we might be New Age and therefore under Satanic influence. Elsewhere, an individual reserved his right to spray aerosol daily proclaiming that the "witches" of Earth Day could not save the world; only God could save the world. Still another declared he burned 500 tires on April 22 just from spite: "Ha, ha, ha!" But these were the exceptions. In the final tally, the letters were optimistic . . . even in the face of some brutal environmental circumstances.

Though no single letter proclaims a grand scheme for our future, the authors all together seem to be pointing towards a new way of living. From the mainstream of America, from foreign shores everywhere, they hope for a time when we become aware of our interconnectedness, when we consider the effects of our behavior on others and other species, and when we act not by compulsion but by choice. The letters speak of a time of conscious living. Igor Shklyarevsky of the Soviet Union captures the prevailing hope of the letters to Earth Day:

I believe there will come a time when the nations will be proud not of their factories and smoggy horizons, but of green leaves, the dew, the coolness of nights, and the scent of mists and marshlands.

I believe these letters proclaim: That time has begun!

Peter Wright
Palo Alto

1. Suited to the Task?

Earth Day is over and the country's most elegant pedestrian mall--Fifth Avenue--is again just another noisy, congested, exhaust-poisoned traffic artery, like all the other streets in this noisy, congested, exhaust-poisoned pollution capital of the world.

Was it all just a passing fancy--the speeches, the clean-ups, the teach-ins, the public promises and private vows to respect and restore the depleted environment in cities, towns and hamlets across an America that is not so beautiful as our forefathers found it?

Is the sudden concern for the environment merely another "nice, good middle-class issue," as one organizer put it, conveniently timed to divert the nation's attention from such pressing problems as the spreading war in Indochina and intractable social injustice at home?

If anything is clear after yesterday's teach-ins it is that restoring purity to the national air and water and rebuilding the cities is going to require enormous expenditures, great changes in every aspect of American life. This reality adds urgency to President Nixon's promise to reduce foreign commitments, especially the costly war in Viet Nam.

Suddenly ecology is on everybody's lips. Concern with ecology is fashionable nowadays. But if the fad dies, we die with it . . .

The New York Times
April 23, 1970

It has been twenty years but all that seems to have changed is the name of the President and the name of the war. Even though more environmental groups have formed, more laws have been passed, and some trends, such as river pollution, have been reversed, the forces at work against the environment have grown even more quickly. The problems are far more complex than twenty years ago and the rate of decay much faster. Way back then we had no Love Canal, no Three-Mile Island, no Chernobyl, no Bhopal, no Exxon Valdez, no ozone depletion, no rainforest destruction, and no massive extinction of species. We fought for clean water and clear air - as though that were all we needed to fight for. Oh, for the good old days!

Solutions now seem farther away. When we try to imagine a future for ourselves, we see that, no matter who wins, good guys or bad guys, we will have less of a world. "What kind of a movie is this?" the average, middle-class citizen might ask. "What kind of story does not have a happy ending? I am not sure I want to be watching." How many people have tuned out because there seems to be no possibility for us to live happily ever after?

As the bodies pile up, and we push boldly forward toward the next century, those concerned with the ethics of a decaying world wrestle with the questions: Is it accident or is it murder? Is someone to blame? Is someone to be punished? Who is to pay? And who is to make these decisions?

In this chapter are letters describing some urgent problems that built up between the two Earth Days, and letters addressing the question: Is Earth Day 1990 suited to the task?

June 1989, Burma -

In ancient times, Burmese armies used elephants to carry troops into battle against other nations. Today, Burma kills elephants in order to finance its war with other nations as well as with political dissidents.

We, the Karens, are an indigenous tribal people of Southeast Asia. Millions of us live in Burma, in the cities, in valley towns, and in forest villages. We respect the natural environment due to beliefs passed down to us from our ancestors. Unfortunately in Burma our forest environment is being besieged by the troops of the military dictatorship of Ne Win and Saw Maung. This regime, which does not hesitate to kill unarmed students, protestors, and tribespeople, is on a rampage to gain control of our forest home and sell out our trees. An appalling feature of this campaign is their greedy trade in endangered species. They care about wildlife even less than about human rights, which is to say: Not at all! Tiger and leopard skins and tortoise shell products have been dealt in openly.

In contrast, even within the stresses of a frontier war, the Karen National Union has outlawed since 1978 the hunting of hornbills, elephants, and rhinoceros. Some of Asia's last examples of endangered species thrive in our liberated zone, Kawthoolei, including tigers, tapirs, rhinoceros, wild ox, leopards, hornbills, peacocks, and wild elephants.

The Karen people are now particularly concerned with the elephants. Asian elephant population during the last part of the 20th Century has dwindled even more than the African elephants, whose plight is now arousing world attention. The Asian elephant is in immediate danger of extinction, and ivory from Asian elephants is supposed to be banned, although the trade continues.

The Karen National Union
Department of Foreign Affairs

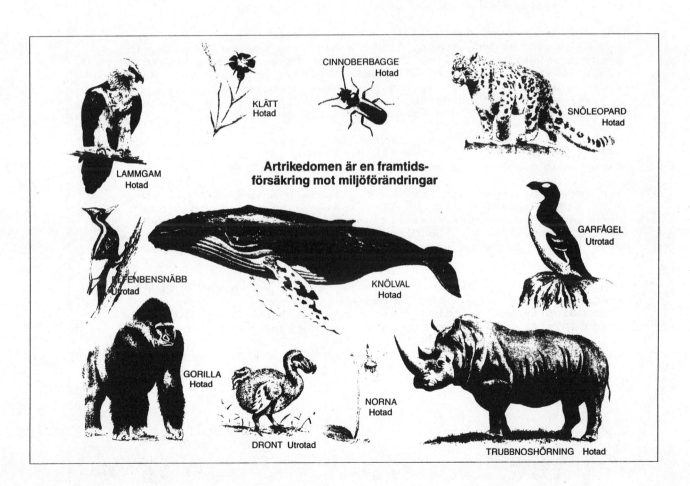

Steffan Ullstrom
ISU AB, Sweden

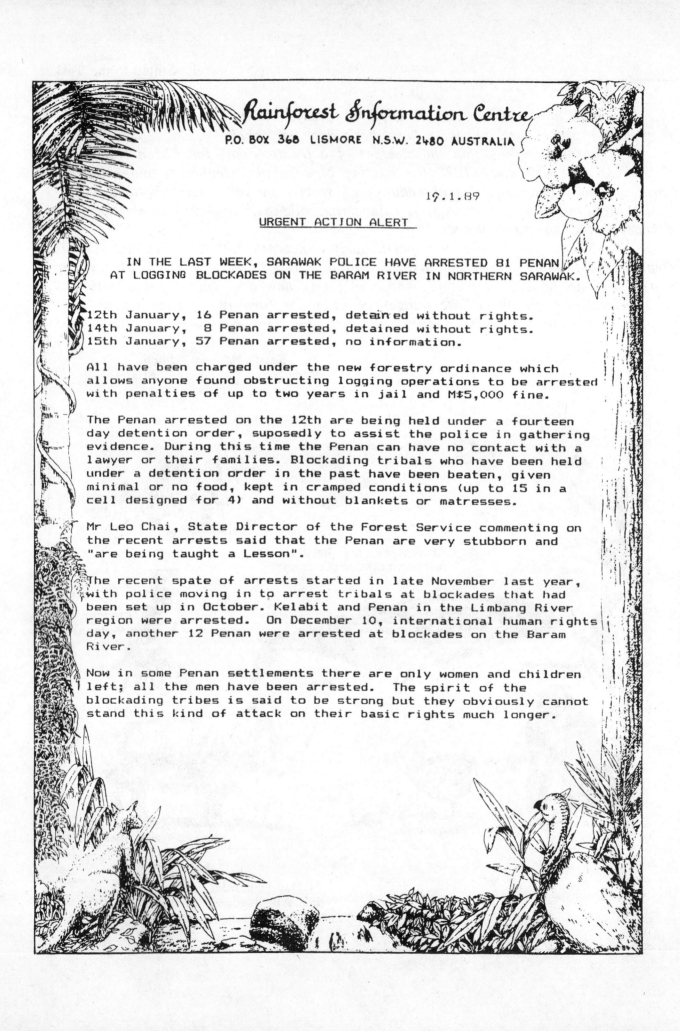

Rainforest Information Centre

P.O. BOX 368 LISMORE N.S.W. 2480 AUSTRALIA

19.1.89

<u>URGENT ACTION ALERT</u>

IN THE LAST WEEK, SARAWAK POLICE HAVE ARRESTED 81 PENAN AT LOGGING BLOCKADES ON THE BARAM RIVER IN NORTHERN SARAWAK.

12th January, 16 Penan arrested, detained without rights.
14th January, 8 Penan arrested, detained without rights.
15th January, 57 Penan arrested, no information.

All have been charged under the new forestry ordinance which allows anyone found obstructing logging operations to be arrested with penalties of up to two years in jail and M$5,000 fine.

The Penan arrested on the 12th are being held under a fourteen day detention order, suposedly to assist the police in gathering evidence. During this time the Penan can have no contact with a lawyer or their families. Blockading tribals who have been held under a detention order in the past have been beaten, given minimal or no food, kept in cramped conditions (up to 15 in a cell designed for 4) and without blankets or matresses.

Mr Leo Chai, State Director of the Forest Service commenting on the recent arrests said that the Penan are very stubborn and "are being taught a Lesson".

The recent spate of arrests started in late November last year, with police moving in to arrest tribals at blockades that had been set up in October. Kelabit and Penan in the Limbang River region were arrested. On December 10, international human rights day, another 12 Penan were arrested at blockades on the Baram River.

Now in some Penan settlements there are only women and children left; all the men have been arrested. The spirit of the blockading tribes is said to be strong but they obviously cannot stand this kind of attack on their basic rights much longer.

October 1989, Philippines -

Samar, our beautiful island, is in crisis. The forests are quickly disappearing, threatened by indiscriminate logging despite a logging ban. Whole communities are threatened by landslides and river bank erosion. Fields are frequently flooded and buried under sand and mud. Further downstream, coral reefs around the island loose their productivity. Fishermen are experiencing declining catch. How will this beautiful island look like, when our generation will finally hand it over to our children?

Council for Development of Samar Island
P. O. Box 46
6710 Calbayog City, Philippines

October, 1989, Brazil -

About the Japanese involvement . . . Japan wanted to finance the paving of BR 364 through Acre (AH-kray) and to link it up with the Peruvian road system, but Bush made it clear at Hirohito's burial that the U.S., having put major pressure on the World Bank and the Inter-American Development Bank not to continue with the BR 364 unless full guarantees for the protection of the environ-ment and the local people would be made, that this would not be appreciated by the U.S.
The Japanese seem to be a little more concerned about their (lack of) ecological image than they used to be, so they have withdrawn their proposal. At the same time, however, they give soft loans to Brazil, which the government can easily use to construct the road themselves, which they seem determined to do. Of course, it is then impossible to control the massive immigration and environmental destruction associated with it. Also, Peru now wants to 'develop' its Amazonia to get out of the debt situation.

European Working Group on Amazonia
Gibraltar

December 1989, Jakarta -

Project Turtles began about one year ago as we, now the 9th grade of the German International School Jakarta, visited a turtle beach. There we saw the turtle eggs being taken away by the "rangers" for the local market. Since then we have taken up contact with other international organizations such as Greenpeace.

We are trying to make the Indonesians be aware of the consequences the turtle slaughter has on the biological balance.

Project Turtles
P.O. Box 2331
Jakarta, Indonesia

In the early 70's I was very involved in Earth Day, as were many fellow hippies. So happy to see a renewed interest in our Mother Earth. There are M's of us interested in this important life-saving cause, but have lost touch since we dropped out and are now living in the wild woods of Texas.

Pauline Shreve-Broussard
30 Martin Drive
Conroe, Texas, USA

© 1969 Atomic Energy Group

The actions you call for and the concern you show is admirable but a decade too late. With terrestrial and aquatic ecosystems on the verge of collapse through extinction of species, greed, pollution, ignorance, or stupidity, (and) in the continued waste of resources at (a) truly monumental scale . . . little time (remains) for small half-hearted measures. You should be more forceful in the types of action and the changes in lifestyle that the world ecosystem requires.

USA

I like your Earth Day 1990 Logo. It would make a great Postage Stamp.

Karen D. H. Warden
Lawrence, Kansas, USA

There can be no power in the square. You will notice that everything an Indian does is in a circle, and that is because the Power of the World always works in circles, and everything tries to be round.

Black Elk

Nature creates in circles and moves in circles . . . The square is the product of logic and rationality. It was invented by civilized man. It is the work of masculine consciousness . . . The whole object of logic is to square the circle. Civilization is a circle squared. That's why in civilized societies women's lot--and Nature's lot--has been such a sorry one.

Tom Robbins

Two above submitted by:
"Dirty Dan, Garden Doctor"
Fayetteville, Arkansas, USA

Japan's Earth Day 1990, in its search for a friendly-looking character, selected "Eartha" by Mr. Tatsuaki Hamada, an artist with a deep and profound respect for Nature. Mr. Hamada sees man as an integral part of Nature and believes that everything that exists is necessary or it wouldn't exist. With "Eartha" he expresses a quiet yet firm love for all living things. The mark symbolizes the antithesis to modern man's sick and misguided approach to the Earth's environment. "Eartha", hugging the earth affectionately in her arms, beckons to us all to reflect on the lunacy of this part of Nature called "man", who has caused so much pain to Earth. "Eartha" carries the message of hope.

Japan

People sense that our planet is in trouble, but most feel helpless in the face of such awesome threats as global warming, ozone holes, rain forest destruction, and other worldwide problems.

Earth Day 1990 is being organized to overcome this sense of despair. It is founded in the belief that people--individually and collectively--do indeed count, and, working together, can accomplish extraordinary things.

The environmental crisis--despite its global scope--is not beyond ken or control. Indeed, the crisis exists precisely because of the actions we have taken and the policies we have adopted. Our species got itself into this mess, and we must get ourselves out of it.

> Australian Conservation Foundation
> 340 Gore Street
> Fitzroy 3065, Australia

I think it's an incredible venture that you're taking on with Earth Day 1990! It's such a hopeful way to bring people together in the struggle against the decadence in our environment. When I read about Earth Day in Not Man Apart, I became totally interested in participating. I'm only a junior in high school, but these problems are so real to me, and when I have children, I want them to grow freely in a SAFE, CLEAN, HEALTHY environment.

I wish I knew effective ways to make the people in my school aware of these problems, but some of them are such dummies and all they do is deplete the ozone layer with hairspray. Please help me help them!

Thank you so much for bringing hope, and I will do my best to help make Earth Day 1990 a reality EVERY DAY!

God bless you all.

> Julia Brandt
> 21 Percy Williams Drive
> East Islip, New York, USA

To,
    The Chairman
    'EART DAY',1990.
    P.O.Box-AA
    STANFORD UNIVERSITY
    CALIFORNIA,94309
    U.S.A

    Subject:Application for joining the 4th comming students confer
            -ence, 'EARTH DAY' , 22nd April, 1990.

Dear Sir,
            With due respect and humble submission, I beg to state th-
-te, Iam a Bangladeshi student of Cost & Management Accounting und-
-er the University of Dhaka. For aquiring much knowledge and give
my valuable opinion and making,good Friendship with the students

of various parts of the world, I want to take part in the 4th comm-
ing students conferece, 'EARTH DAY'held in 22nd April , 1990.

        Therefore, I hope that your honour would be kind enough to co-
-operate and send me the invitation letter and other formalities
and forward my application . With a lot of thanks.

                                        Sincerely yours

                                        (MD.PERVEZ SAJJAD)

To day's date:
02Dec,1989.

                        MD Pervez Sajjad
                        32-B (old) Azimpur State
                        Azimpur, Dhaka, Bangladesh

I am interested in helping to make Earth Day 1990 the largest demonstration in human history . . . Please let me know of your current plans so the information can get to everyone . . . I want this to be a statement to the present and future leaders of the world that grassroots support of our natural environment is without parallel in the history of man.

Daniel L. Swan
UNC Campus Area Coordinator
Greensboro, North Carolina, USA

Saint Louis, Missouri

I don't know if it has finally come to the point (at which) people cannot ignore that we have a problem, or that celebrities, actors and actresses, MTV coverage, etc. are getting media coverage--therefore so is the problem--whatever it is, whatever works--as long as people are made aware that we do have a problem and clean it up!

Debbe Villagran
Arlington, Texas, USA

I pledge to do my utmost to stamp out these ineffective, self-serving publicity campaigns that waste true environmental contributions. I am a professional environmentalist; (it's) my life's work. Millions for earth's defense; not one cent for tribute.

Dwight Frye
2303 Carnegie Lane #G
Redondo Beach, California   USA

European Television Company
etc.

France

Meanwhile, know that everywhere I go, people are talking about Earth Day. Like German Unity, Earth Day is at the forefront of everyone's consciousness in these early months of 1990. That's your real success. Congratulations!

David R. Woollcombe, President
Peace Child International
Postbus 772
1200 AT Hilversum
The Netherlands

I am surprised at the lack of publicity so far and am concerned that if too much more time passes, Earth Day will wind up as a "flash in the pan" instead of a thought-provoking, consciousness-raising event.

Raymond P. Saracino
Syracuse, New York, USA

It goes without saying that we lack the use of the media that is so vital to such a program and it would be to our advantage if we could place more emphasis in this direction.

MD Mozammel Haque, Director
United Club, G.P.O. Box 2296
Dhaka-1000, Bangladesh

I donate money once a year in December. Please "remind" me of your good works then, but only then. The frequency of your letters does not impress me as to the urgency of your cause. If there is a crisis in your world, please don't use it as a P.R. tool. You're in the business of handling crisis. My local fire department doesn't ask for more money just after each fire.

John T. Howard
The Knolls
South Hadley, Massachusetts, USA

My heart and soul go out to you and yours for such an uplifting and motivating idea . . . to give the world a chance to express concern for the protection of our earth . . .
Keep loving this god-given earth as much as I do!
In Highest Regards & Praise for All Your Efforts.

Mrs. Ann Doby Mercer
Rt 1, Box 446-A
Hamlet, North Carolina, USA

Thank you for sending my order of Earth Day bumper stickers. They are well done and I'm sure people will want to buy them.
However, there is some irony in the fact that Earth Day bumper stickers came in styrofoam pellets. Packing your materials in a more organic substance would help promote consideration for the earth.

Barbara Veranian
Sandpoint, Idaho, USA

While I share your concern, I have decided to contribute exclusively to those organizations to whom global freedom from pollution is evidenced in abstaining from use of the see-through envelopes which cannot be recycled.

Helga Aschaffenburg
Medford Leas 285
Medford, New Jersey, USA

I know the personal sacrifice and commitment required to take on a project of this magnitude and I applaud your efforts.

> Joy W. Shortell
> Cayuga Comm College
> Franklin Street
> Auburn, New York, USA

I've just read of your great efforts and my heart is lightened to know that people are uniting to save our precious environment and wildlife.

> Linda Graves
> 201 Northview Drive
> Chesapeake, Virginia, USA

I am writing to express my deep disappointment that meat was being sold at the Earth Day 1990 festival in San Francisco's Chrissy Field. On a day dedicated to the awakening of people's consciousness about planetary issues, it was an irony to see meat being sold and consumed. Even without taking into account the incredible cruelty and abuse that went into making that meat, a meat-based diet is not an environmentally sound diet.

Earth Day was an opportunity for its organizers and participants to truly make a meaningful statement. Instead, it was just another fair, albeit much more crowded and trashy.

> Lina M. Alta
> 456 Montgomery Street 16th Floor
> San Francisco, California, USA

Thanks for the incentive to get off my butt and do something about what I've been thinking about for years! All I needed was a vehicle and Earth Day serves that purpose.

> Karen Whittlesey Anderson
> Forest Falls, California, USA

I am quite appalled at the deterioration of the earth and I am proud to see such a group of citizens doing their jobs as they should be done.

Bradly Lee Vance
40 Saunders Road S.E.
Kalkaska, Michigan, USA

Thank you, not only for the information but simply for being. Because of people like you, my children may still have a beautiful world to grow up in.

Carey Watzka
De Pere, Wisconsin, USA

There is good in the world when there is Earth Day 1990. Thus, there shall be good at Cal Poly (or anywhere else) when Earth Day is there, too.

Eric Strain
San Luis Obispo, California, USA

O.K., you've piqued my curiosity. WHAT IS EARTH DAY 1990?

Sean Ramirez
11921 Sackston Ridge
St. Louis, Missouri, USA

Earth Day is a fabulous idea for those of us who want to be actively involved but don't have an outlet!

Carol Anne Herren
Richmond, Virginia, USA

BOUM BOUM, PAS BOUM

OU

PREPARER LE FUTUR

Reconnaître l'existence d'un problème est le premier pas vers la recherche de sa solution.

Cette première fiche n'est pas dédiée à un seul problème mais nous donne la méthode pour les affronter tous.

Cette méthode comprend plusieurs étapes :
- reconnaître le problème
- en découvrir les origines
- rechercher les solutions pour le résoudre
- les mettre en pratique

La bombe représente l'ensemble des situations explosives qui intéressent notre environnement et que nous devons affronter le plus vite possible afin d'éviter notre propre destruction.

KEEP THE EARTH ALIVE

BEST WISH IS
FROM A LITTLE
HUNGARIAN VILLAGE
KISDOROG

2.   From Everywhere, From Everyone

The variety of letters made turning to the next one exciting. They came from the University of Tehran and from Tender Sprouts Nursery School, from Tom Cruise and Bill Walsh, from the Mayor of New York and the Prime Minister of Australia. They came from 140 countries, from every continent, from islands and atolls around the globe. While some authors felt called on to add something practically or philosophically to a movement, others simply sensed an open door through which to march with their emotions. All wanted to be connected with this event. From her own need to participate, Captain R. S. Hellman, a United States Marine stationed in Okinawa, wrote. Triphonas Topalides, from a small village of northern Greece, sent in her support. Petra Dimpfel wanted to take part. Her group lives in Norden, a little town in Ostfriesland, coast of North Sea. And Ellen Pollack shared "We in the Bronx are concerned, too." Something told them that no longer was environmental concern a small breeze, but a great wind that touched everyone everywhere; they all wanted to be sailing on that wind.

In this chapter are the letters that do not fit elsewhere. Their vitality, like all the letters of the book, speaks for the resilience of a species not giving itself over to oblivion.

I am the scoutmaster of the Grupo 228 "Gabriel Cuervo Salcedo". The Group is composed of 50 boys and girls from a little town named Guatavita, one and a half hours away from Bogota.

Actually, we have the problem, that the town is surrounded by hills in an advanced state of erosion, to the point that there are many square miles that have almost transformed into desert.

Since the foundation of our Scout Group we have been making a campaign in order to save the soil and reestablish the former forests.

Rainer   Dillmann
Guatavita, Colombia

The vegetal landscape of the Azores is dominated by exotic plants that have colonized extensively all the islands. The native vegetation, that contains a large number of plants not found in other parts of the world (endemic species), is widely dispersed, occupying small residual areas that are rapidly disappearing.

Even the most valuable plant community, the Juniperus-Laurus forest, rich in endemic plants derived from a remote extinct European flora, is severely threatened. It is a relict ecosystem of high biological diversity, with international importance, which has not been fully investigated. The critical situation of the Azorean flora is made plain by the inclusion of 73% of the 56 endemic species in the list of rare and threatened . . . plants . . . 19 of these plants now face the risk of extinction.

Quercus/Acores
Project Azorica
P.O. Box 124
9900 Horta, Portugal

The Karens prefer to be called "a nationality" or "indigenous people", but they can also be properly called "tribal" or "a tribe" . . . There are some three million Karens in Burma, and more living in Thailand. Burma's Karens are animists, Buddhists, and Baptists. They won fame as guerilla fighters on the Allied side in World War II, and have produced noted teachers, missionaries, and doctors. Currently, their forest territory has been subjected to extremely heavy warfare in the "Teak War" . . . and over 20,000 Karens are refugees in Thailand. A Karen elephant sanctuary is in particular danger from the warfare. The Karens are renowned elephant trainers and mahouts, culturally bonded with elephants.

The way things are in Thailand these days, I think it's best not to give a phone contact.

Edith T. Mirante
Project Maje
14 Dartmouth Road
Cranford, New Jersey, USA

Our country is yet young and our feeling is that of optimism for the creation of a healthy people with a sound natural resource management. The decade of the 90's for sure can threaten our unique environment, but for sure, there (also) lies hope. . . we lack finance, (but) we will celebrate Earthday 1990 using raw materials at hand in order to create an awareness (and) concern . . .

We remain yours as one together for a better environment and people on Earth.

Youth Environmental Action
San Jose Succotz
Cayo District, Belize

Yes, we are a bit late getting this to you (but time is relative, Einstein said), and no, this isn't recycled paper (we ran out a few days back), but still, we thought you folks should know that the environmental movement is alive and kicking down here among the rednecks.

Susan D. Branton
Students for Environmental Awareness
Box 2460 University Station
Clemson, South Carolina, USA

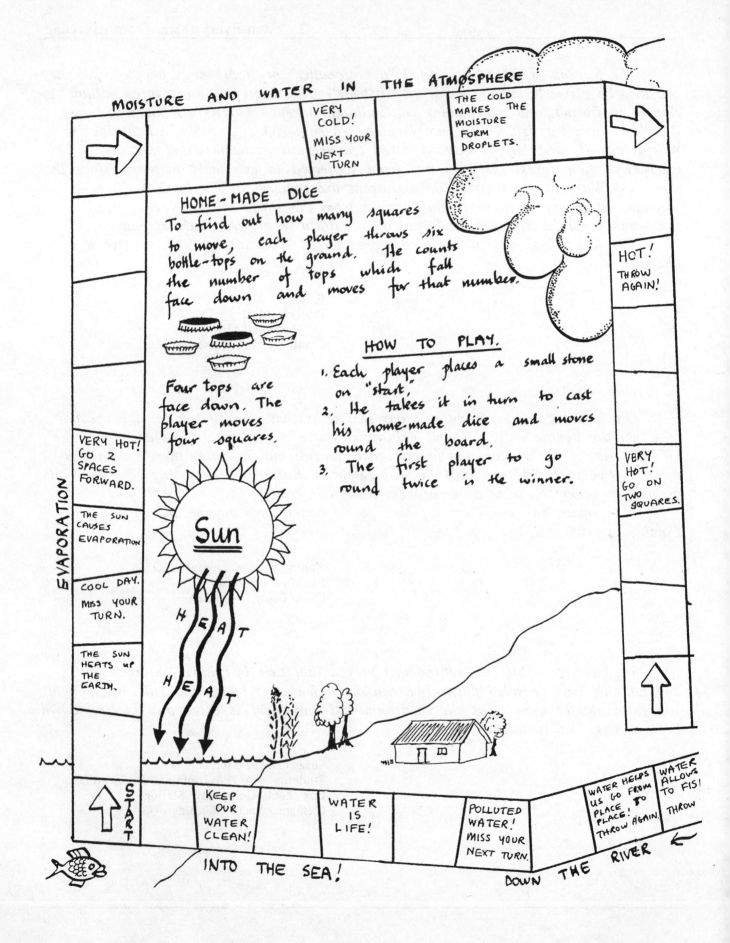

MOISTURE AND WATER IN THE ATMOSPHERE

VERY COLD! MISS YOUR NEXT TURN

THE COLD MAKES THE MOISTURE FORM DROPLETS.

HOT! THROW AGAIN!

HOME-MADE DICE

To find out how many squares to move, each player throws six bottle-tops on the ground. He counts the number of tops which fall face down and moves for that number.

HOW TO PLAY.

1. Each player places a small stone on "start".
2. He takes it in turn to cast his home-made dice and moves round the board.
3. The first player to go round twice is the winner.

Four tops are face down. The player moves four squares.

Sun

H E A T

H E A T

VERY HOT! GO 2 SPACES FORWARD.

THE SUN CAUSES EVAPORATION

COOL DAY. MISS YOUR TURN.

THE SUN HEATS UP THE EARTH.

EVAPORATION

VERY HOT! GO ON TWO SQUARES.

START

KEEP OUR WATER CLEAN!

WATER IS LIFE!

POLLUTED WATER! MISS YOUR NEXT TURN.

WATER HELPS US GO FROM PLACE TO PLACE! THROW AGAIN.

WATER ALLOWS TO FISH THROW

INTO THE SEA!

DOWN THE RIVER

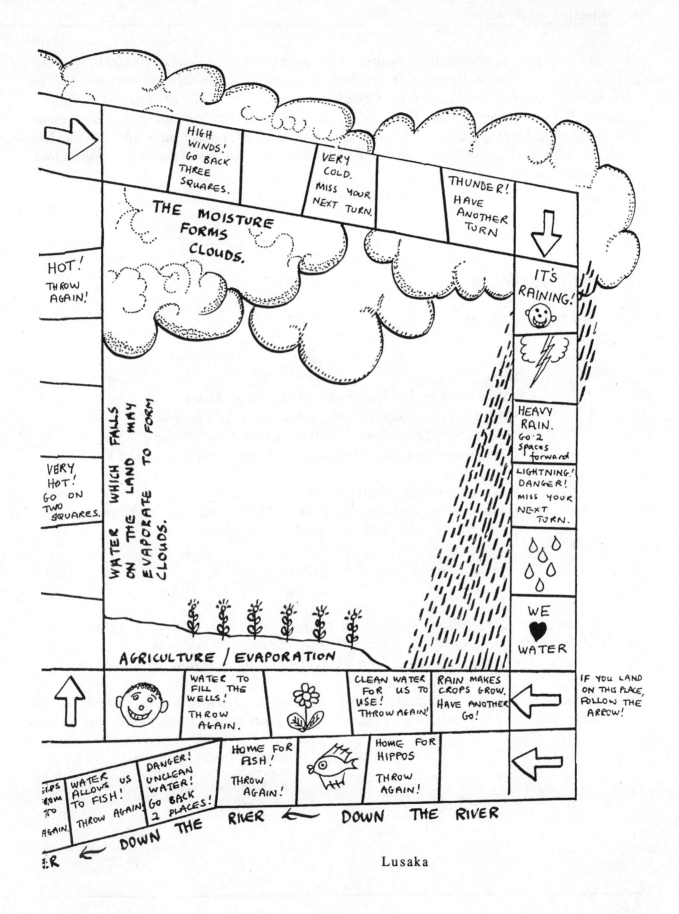

Lusaka

Thank you for including information about Environmental Protection Club of Latvia (VAK) in your January/December International Update. However, I must respectfully request that in future Updates you not list VAK or Latvia in the Country Report under USSR. VAK since its inception has always been very clear that it does not recognize the de jure incorporation of Latvia into the Soviet Union. I realize that this may seem a small detail, but . . . we would greatly appreciate your cooperation.

Latvia

LET THERE (BE) PEACE
DEEP LIKE A RIVER
LET THERE (BE) DREAMS
FILLING THE SKY

Name: *Toryu*
Address: *The Endless Path of the Yogi Monk*
City: *Global Village;* State: *Samadhi;* Zip: *The Future*
Telephone: *Late 20th Century Earth/Gaia/Mother Ship*
I am interested in volunteering. Please contact me. *I've been contacted*
K-12 or College Student: *Student of Life*
I am also supporting Earth Day 1990 with my contribution: *My Life Body which will both die and live forever.*

I am a primary school teacher in remote south-west Nepal. I know, and periodically hold meetings for, about 12 surrounding primary school principals. Send us any information or ideas you think would be relevant to small rural schools and I'll share that with them.

Regardless, I will encourage all of them to start using waste baskets in the classrooms and to start compost heaps . . . At present it's thrown out the window.

Damian Jones, Volunteer
American Peace Corps
Kathmandu, Nepal

Depto de Biologia, C.U.E.G.

UNIVERSIDAD NACIONAL AUTONOMA DE HONDURAS
CIUDAD UNIVERSITARIA
TEGUCIGALPA, D. C., HONDURAS, C. A.

March 12, 1990

Owen Byrd
Earth Day 1990
P.O. Box AA
Stanford, Ca.   94309

Dear Mr. Owen:

Twenty years ago, when I was a graduate student in Zoology at the University of Maryland I participated in the first Earth Day. This year I would like to participate again, with the help of my students at the Universidad Nacional Autonoma de Honduras (National University of Honduras). It is the only government university in Honduras and has around 30,000 students.

Yesterday a friend lent me a copy of the "Campus Environmental Audit" which I found very interesting and worthwhile, but defenitely tuned to U.S. universities.

For instance, Honduras has no environmental laws and there is no environmental office on the campus to coordinate complaints and to take action. As a case in point, the trash from the biological sciences building is tossed in heaps by the side of the building next to my lab, where the constant wind blows it around. Eventually, it is burned. Recently, when my students and I were returning from a field study, one of the girls jabbed her foot and drew blood through her soft tennis shoe with a used hypodermic needle in which there were traces of blood. This needle was part of the solid waste from the health center which is located in the biological sciences building. We immediately went to the health center and were told not to worry because there had been no cases of AIDS or hepatitis that week. They finally agreed to dispose of the used needles more carefully but, unfortunately, they are not complying.

Becky Myton
Dr. Becky Myton

Becky Myton
Depto. de Biologia, C.U.E.G.,
Universidad Nacional Autonoma de Hondura
Tegucigalpa, Honduras

I have to admit, I got your address from a comic book. You know, the little ads that have been published in DC COMICS . . . with Superman standing by our beloved home and the caption, "Be A Hero. Save the World" . . . I am 16 and I am inheriting the Earth from you adults. I want a clean and healthy Earth . . . In my school a bunch of friends and I have formed an awareness group . . . We don't get as much done as we would like, but every little bit helps, right? . . . The planet Earth is a frail place, and it's up to the creatures that fouled it up, namely human beings, to help fix the damage wrought. Thank you for organizing Earth Day. Our world needs and appreciates it.

Tad C. Ellsworth
1721 30th Street N.W.
Canton, Ohio, USA

Cheng Rickey Xiang
Fresno, California, USA

Earth Day 1990
4/8/90

To Who ever it may concern

    Could you please send me some information about becoming a hero, I've always read comics, both Marvel and D.C. So you see I have some ideal about what being a hero is, and in my own way I am already a super secret hero.

    What I need is a way to make money being a hero. Being a hero and getting paid chicken fee is no fun, Espicallialy with what I Do.

Sincerly Yours

Joseph M. Weathersby

Better Known as
* MARACtus *

Joseph Marcus Weathersby
245 Earnshaw
Cincinnati, Ohio, USA

(Our) Mediterranean area benefits from a benign climate and offers some enviable living conditions. On the other hand, its basic resources are very fragile. The soil is poor and the water scarce. Barcelona is reaching its limits of water supply. Sixty percent of Catalunya runs the risk of thirst in case of a drought without prospects of solution from outside water sources. Despite this, the majority of the scanty rivers are open sewages. The forestry policy is a chaos; the public works, especially the roads and motorways, are defacing the entire landscape; quarries and mines are being opened and closed without any compliance with existing regulations; rubbish and industrial residues pose problems which remain unsolved. Catalunya is the area with most nuclear power plants in all of Spain. Unfortunately, and despite the political speeches, our land is a victim of all the major problems that scandalize us at the universal level.

Spain

There can now be little doubt that the situation facing these ancient animals in the Mediterranean is grave in the extreme, yet, despite the various research programmes, political debates, and paper protection measures of the 1980's, their plight continues to worsen year by year.

The sole purpose of MEDASSET is to rationalize and update the conservation requirements for Marine Turtles in the Mediterranean . . . and to assess and advise on . . . the rather repetitious meetings and symposia which serve more to publicize researches than to apply results.

Lily Venizelos, MEDASSET Steering Committee
Mediterranean Assn. to Save the Sea Turtles
c/o Daphne Corp
24 Park Towers - 2 Brick Street
London W1 7DF, England

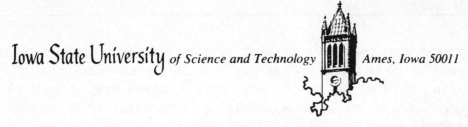

Iowa State University *of Science and Technology*   Ames, Iowa 50011

CHANGING THE ORBIT AND THE TILT OF THE EARTH BY LANDING THE MOON ON THE EARTH. ALSO ALTERING THE SOLAR SYSTEM

To solve the enormous climatic and ecological problems which are increasingly threatening mankind's general welfare as well as its very existence, radical and bold methods must be implemented which go beyond the traditionally regional ones.

The ecology of the planet Earth is inextricably related to the cosmic trajectory (including the orbit) and the tilt of the Earth and to the setup of the entire Solar System.

There is no reason to believe or to take for granted that the existing orbit of the planet Earth and its tilt and the existing setup of the Solar System are the optimal ones as far as the ecology of the Earth is concerned.

A judicious change of the tilt or of the orbit of the Earth or a judicious alteration of the Solar System will most radically improve the ecology of the planet Earth and the quality of life on Earth.

The changes in Solar System can be performed by altering the orbits of the planets Mercury, Venus and Mars or by combining some of these or other planets into one or by fragmenting them.

For an earlier implementation of the radical ecological changes the way is to focus on the Moon.

The present-day technology is adequate to perform: (1) a partial reduction of the mass of the Moon, or (2) a splitting of the Moon into two or more pieces, or (3) a controlled total elimination of the Moon, or (4) a change of the orbit of the Moon with a change of the distance of the Moon from the Earth, or (5) landing a part or parts or the entire Moon on the Earth.

The preliminary indications are that in all of the cases (1), (2), (3), (4), (5), the cosmic trajectory of the Earth and its tilt could be so altered as to have a most beneficial effect on the global ecology of the Earth. <u>The landing of a part or parts or the entire Moon on the Earth (especially in the Pacific Ocean, near the South Pole) is by far a most efficient technique for altering the tilt of the Earth.</u>

Computerized simulation of the cases ranging from (1) to (5) will determine the course of the action for obtaining optimal results.

It seems inevitable that the genius of mankind will not tolerate not having a direct and total control over the cosmic trajectory of the planet Earth. Also, it seems inevitable that the genius of mankind will not tolerate being hostage to the Earth's existing orbit forever or not having any control over the setup of the Solar System.

Sincerely,

Alexander Abian

Alexander Abian
Professor of Mathematics

Living on the east coast doesn't alert people to what is happening to our planet. The ocean is always green from the New Jersey chemical plants, and the people are already dead as far as I'm concerned. I tried doing something with "Save the Whales". There are so many homeless, who cares about the whales? This is a normal attitude here.

L. M. P.
Brooklyn, New York, USA

Istvan   Lehocki
Uj Ludas Mgz., Hungary

Hi! This is Donna and I am not happy with the way my school is handling the recycling process. Our lunches are served in recyclable styrofoam but they are thrown in with all the other trash. Let's say only 300 of our 1500 students eat those lunches: 1500 trays a week, 54,000 a year! Sickening! The amounts of aluminum cans, paper bags, and plastics are overwhelming. We're throwing it all AWAY!

Donna Braquet
Slidell, Louisiana, USA

Hello. My name is Megan Culler and I am . . . worried about the major trash problem. One of my classmates said "Why don't we throw all the trash in the volcanoes of the earth." Another said "Why don't we give it to Asia. They have plenty of room."

Megan Ann Culler
2244 Gnarled Pine Dr.
Dublin, Ohio, USA

March 17, 1990

Celebrate Earth Day
P.O. Box AA
Stanford University
Stanford, CA 94309

Dear Sir:

My name is Lorna Tokar. I am 12 yrs. old. I am in the 5th grade at Wheeless Road Elementary School in Augusta, GA.

For Earth Day, I have to give a report in school. Everyone has a partner except me - I think. I wanted to do this myself. My report will be on trash pollution. Will you please help me and send me some information and pictures on pollution and what Earth Day is all about. I have cerebral palsy and I want to do a good job.

Lorna Tokar
(Lorna Tokar)
2809 Rocky Creek Road
Augusta, GA 30906

I am a typical Texas housewife with one child. I have recently begun recycling my everyday waste. I have never worn fur and have cut beef down to twice a week in our diets. This was not easy considering my husband does not really like chicken or fish. I am considering talking to my neighbors about letting me recycle for them. I intend to do this within a week or two.

However, I have a much larger concern. My husband and I own a tire shop at which we sell hundreds of tires per month. Several of our family and friends face the same problem: there is no place for the old tires. I know of no way or place to recycle tires or dispose of them in an environmentally safe manner. Currently we take them to the city land fills. We are a small establishment and probably dump 400 tires a month. I know of larger places that dump at least 1,500 or more per month and this worries me. . . what can I do about it?

Mamie Fording
3114 Catalpa
Garland, Texas, USA

Bowling Green Elementary is alive with beautiful flowering plants and trees. Colorful hanging baskets of flowers line the entire covered walk from Kindergarten to 5th grade . . . Green paper chains denote signatures of those who support the (Green Pledge) effort and join in by promising to help conserve. These long chains hang in profusion in the classrooms where students have collected the signatures. Students numbered the links. Many teachers used the chains to teach fractions, decimals, and percentages.

USA

I got hold of a magazine that has your address printed. So here I am writing. I'm not exactly an "ecologist", nor even anyone linked to a science of ecology. I'm simply an ordinary worker, an "everyday man." Yet I'm disturbed deeply by the enormous weight of problems facing my country, and one of which is ecologic in nature. I would like to be informed about this situation, and have an idea as to how I can be of help no matter how simple as far as my daily life allows me. Perhaps you can send me something to read.

Certainly you are aware of how, in my country, forests are almost finished, corals in seas are bare, etc., etc. ad nauseam. But I'm not despairing.

Hoping for your kind consideration.

Francisco C. Castro
Manila, Philippines

Hello!

USSR, 198904, Ленинград
Ст. Петергоф, 23-КВАРТАЛ
УЛ. Ботаническая 18/3/44
Борисовой Марине

My name's Marina Borisova.
I'm fifteen. I'm from Russia.
I'm writing to you because
I'm trouble about oecology on
our Earth. I'm for the green
peace and clear sky. And I
want everybody to understand
that people can live only in
clear and beautiful peace.
I love drawing, so I send you
some pictures on the theme
oecology and our life in
the whole. In my pictures
I'm trying to show the beauty
of the peace.
I hope you like them.
Please, write me your
opinion on them.

With best wishes

Marina Borisova.
Good-bye.

P.S. Forgive my
mistakes.

Karol Cizmazia
Czechoslovakia

3.   But Why the Trees?

No issue brought more mail. No issue evoked more concern. No issue continues to witness greater visible destruction. No issue needs more immediate action. And none is more easily solved than the horrifying destruction of the tropical rainforests. An irreversible loss of trees and species! Not doing anybody any harm. Just good. So why not bulldoze them and then torch them!? This is ugly and has got to be stopped.

In my advanced English class we had to do a speech on something we were interested in. I did the Rain Forests. At first I thought "Nobody will listen." But when I gave my speech on how the forests are being burned down, everyone turned to listen and really paid attention.

Sarah   Konopik
Omaha, Nebraska, USA

The process of destruction of the rainforests is one of the most serious ecological problems of our time. The destruction of these ecosystems has grave consequences, since it seriously affects, among other things, the climatic equilibrium, accelerates the "greenhouse" effect, and is eliminating one of the most important biological reserves of our planet.

The Amazonian Region contains half of the rainforest areas of the world. In an attempt to formulate a global policy for the region, in 1978, the eight countries that constitute Amazonia (Brazil, Colombia, Venezuela, Ecuador, Peru, Bolivia, Guyana, and Surinam) signed the Treaty for Amazonian Cooperation, but very little has been done for its implementation.

Youth Action for the Defense of the Amazon
Manaus, Brazil

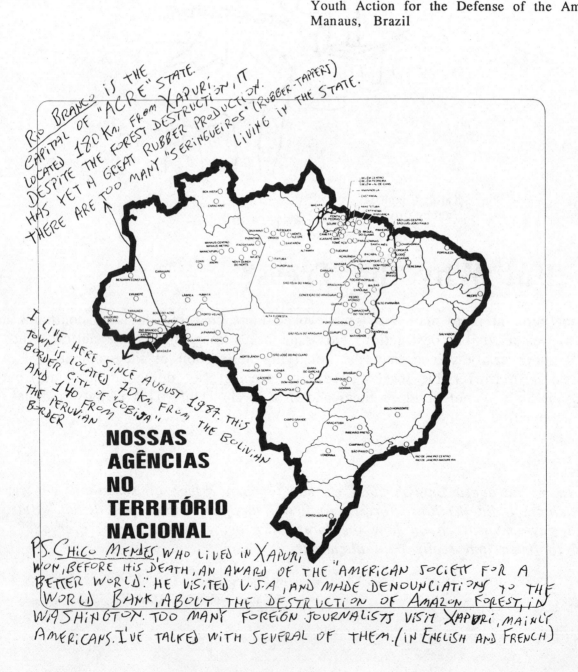

RIO BRANCO IS THE CAPITAL OF "ACRE" STATE. LOCATED 180 Km. FROM XAPURI. DESPITE THE FOREST DESTRUCTION, IT HAS YET A GREAT RUBBER PRODUCTION. THERE ARE TOO MANY "SERINGUEIROS" (RUBBER-TAPPERS) LIVING IN THE STATE.

I LIVE HERE SINCE AUGUST 1987. THIS TOWN IS LOCATED 70 Km FROM THE BOLIVIAN BORDER CITY OF "COBIJA" AND 140 FROM THE PERUVIAN BORDER

NOSSAS AGÊNCIAS NO TERRITÓRIO NACIONAL

P.S. CHICO MENDES, WHO LIVED IN XAPURI WON, BEFORE HIS DEATH, AN AWARD OF THE "AMERICAN SOCIETY FOR A BETTER WORLD." HE VISITED U.S.A, AND MADE DENOUNCIATIONS TO THE WORLD BANK, ABOUT THE DESTRUCTION OF AMAZON FOREST, IN WASHINGTON. TOO MANY FOREIGN JOURNALISTS VISIT XAPURI, MAINLY AMERICANS. I'VE TALKED WITH SEVERAL OF THEM. (IN ENGLISH AND FRENCH)

SECRETARIA DE ESTADO DE SAÚDE

MARCH 19, 1990

TO EARTH DAY 1990

Hi,

I HEARD ABOUT THIS ENTITY FROM A FRIEND OF MINE. I READ IN A LETTER YOU SENT TO HER, THAT YOU'RE GOING TO DO AN EVENT ON APRIL 22, 1990.

WELL, MY NAME IS EDUARDO, I'M A DENTIST WHO LIVE AND WORK ON A LITTLE TOWN OF AMAZON REGION, CALLED XAPURI, A TOWN YOU MUST HAVE BEEN TOLD ABOUT, BECAUSE HERE LIVED AN ECOLOGICAL HERO, A RUBBER-TAPPER WHO FOUGHT AGAINST THE FOREST DESTRUCTION, HIS NAME, CHICO MENDES, KILLED COWARDLY, HERE IN XAPURI, AT DECEMBER 1988.

AS A PERSON WORRIED ABOUT THE CONSERVATION OF THIS DEPLETED REGION, I WOULD LIKE TO KNOW HOW CAN I HELP, AND PARTICIPATE ON THE EVENT YOU'RE GOING TO MAKE ON APRIL 22, 1990. MY NAME AND ADRESS IS:

EDUARDO DE SOUZA
CAIXA POSTAL, 22
69920 XAPURI-AC
BRASIL

I'LL BE WAITING FOR YOU. I'M SENDING INCLUDED A LITTLE MAP SHOWING WHERE I LIVE.

THANKS FOR ATTENTION,

Ed

In Brazil, the general population is not informed about the reality of the deforestation and mercury poisoning in rivers. I need to work fast together with other organizations to alert about the dangers and about the imminent destruction. I believe in what I am doing and I believe in my fellow man.

Instituto de Protecao E. Educacao.
Ambiental "Mendes Santos", Acre, Brazil

Scientists anticipate that if we continue to cut down the tropical rain forests at the present rate for a further six or seven years, then they will be damaged beyond their powers of recovery. Should that happen, the desertification of the tropical regions, and the consequent global warming . . . will render life on this Earth impossible. For the Earth to lose its tropical rain forests is like the human body losing its lungs. Such is the severity of the crisis that we face today.

There are very many Japanese companies among the companies that are responsible for the destruction of the rain forests. Japan imports about half the timber that is traded on the world markets. This is because we consume so much paper and plywood in this country.

Take a box of cookies. Each cookie is itself individually wrapped. When the customer buys it, the shop assistant will again wrap it in beautiful paper, and then she will place it in a paper carrier bag. In Japan we consider such things to be 'good service' on the part of the shops. Alas, for the paper that we here waste so extravagantly, formerly stood as trees in the tropical jungle

The Kumamoto Earth Day Committee
YMCA International Center
12-24 Hanabata Cho, 860 Kumamoto Shi
Japan

I am an eighth grade student from Hardyston, New Jersey. Before Earth Day, I had thought that environmentalism was a noble cause, but not all that important or urgent. Now I realize how very wrong I was . . . One thing that really upsets me are the reports about the destruction of the Amazon rain forest in Brazil. It is totally beyond me how people can be so utterly stupid as to do something like that. Will they ever learn?

Jeremy M. Stevens
Hamburg, New Jersey, USA

Guatemala is under great threat of losing large areas of its tropical conifer forests. This situation can change our country that has been known as "land of eternal spring" into one of "silent spring." To prevent this, we are calling on you, requesting your URGENT SUPPORT.

A paper pulp plant (CELGUSA) is planned to start functioning very shortly, demanding for its operation the . . . natural conifer forests as raw material . . . started in 1977, the plant never functioned, as it was cancelled based upon an environmental impact assessment . . . that showed very serious impact on the environment, natural resources, and the people, as follows:

1. Irreversible loss of 6,500 Ha. per year of natural conifer forests, additional to the present deforestation rate of Guatemala of 1.5 million Ha.

2. Considerable decrease in the water flow in the rivers in the affected areas, especially the Motagua River that runs across the driest valley in Central America. This will have a direct effect on local communities (native populations: irrigation for agriculture and cattle) and contaminate the Atlantic (Caribbean Sea).

3. Negative impact on the climate of the whole region with its consequent effect on global warming.

4. Serious damage to the natural resources of areas such as Sierra de las Minas--known as one of the most important genetic pools in Central America as it contains 70% of the biological diversity of Guatemala.

5. Degradation of these soils as they are highly susceptible to erosion due to the steep topography of the area, with consequent silting of rivers . . .

At present the Spanish government is pressing the Guatemalan government to . . . convert the private, CELGUSA debt (owed to Spain) into a public debt to be paid by the people of Guatemala, (and) . . . to start the plant immediately in order to pay the debt.

The Spanish Ambassador argues that if Guatemala does not agree, the ECC will withdraw all technical and financial cooperation from Guatemala.

We request your support.

1. Request the King and government of Spain to condone a swap of debt for nature.

2. Request the President of Gautemala, Dr. Marco Vinicio Cerezo, not to authorize CELGUSA.

3. Request the President and Congress of Guatemala not to convert the debt from a private one to a public one.

Asociation Guatemalteca Pro Defensa del Medio
Ambiente, Guatemala

March 8 1970

Dear Sir,

Stop cutting down trees perhaps in the future there will be no trees, then there will be no fresh air so stop cutting down trees.

Your frend
Eric

Eric Thomas Shea
Irving, Texas, USA

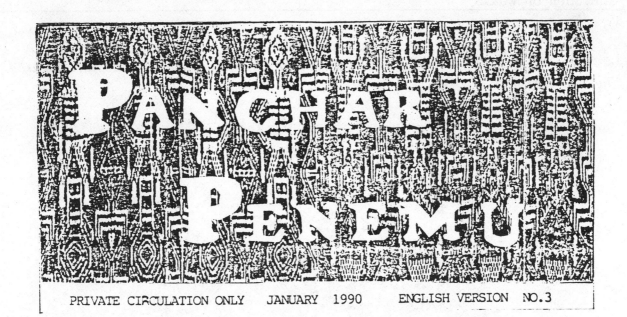

PRIVATE CIRCULATION ONLY   JANUARY 1990   ENGLISH VERSION   NO.3

EDITORIAL

As we usher into the year 1990, let us remember that the problems and issues of the 1980s are still with us: the forest continues to be cut indiscriminately, the workers deaths amounted to a record high of 94 in 17 years while the log production increased steadily; laws that prevent the natives from defending their forest remained unchanged; in certain areas timber companies refused to compensate the destruction caused by logging on their farmlands; our democratic rights remained curbed with the demolishment of the writ of Habeas Corpus in the infamous Internal Security Act, the judiciary have to kow-tow to the executive branch of our government; shifting cultivators are still made the scapegoat of the wanton destruction of Sarawak's rainforest.

An ordinary Sarawakian would ask, "Why do we ordinary people have to suffer, why are we still poor in such a resource-rich country?" The whys are really important if we were to solve our problems as we approach the year 2,000. If we are not part of the solution, we will be still part of the problem. Our lives, whether in the urban or rural area, are inter-related. It is in this inter-relatedness that we seek solidarity with each other to build a progressive and prosperous nation for all.

TO OUR READERS,

WE WISH YOU A HAPPY AND CHALLENGING NEW YEAR 1990 !!!!!!

Institute for Community Education
Sarawak (Borneo), Malaysia

I once dreamed of visions of elven people chatting and dancing all the day long. Their home was the forest. That dream has since dissipated. The forests are fading out fast.

USA

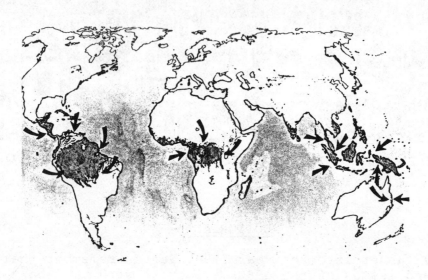

Michael Boston
ISU AB, Sweden

I watch a lot of Public Television, and though they've shown me the beauty of the world, they've also shown me such atrocities as the Exxon oil spill and the destruction of the Amazon Rain Forests. What can I, as a middle class girl from a small Midwest town, do to combat horrors like these?

Angela Costello
Carleton, Michigan, USA

This coming rainy season (June-September) more than 2,000 people have pledged to support us (manpower) in planting 1 million trees different denuded watershed areas of Negros Island. So far, Negros has only 3% remaining forest which is very far from the 40% ecological standard.

Roem L. Delleva, President, Friends of the
Wilderness for Tropical Rainforest Campaign
P.O. Box 313, Bacolod City 6100
Philippines   (Tel. 8-34-43, 5-73-58)

Carlos Vargas . . . is president of the federation of Amazonian Indians, CONFENNAI, and to all intents and purposes has become an able and colorful ambassador. He has successfully managed to reveal the current genocide being inflicted on the Hurani of the Oriente. I will leave it to Douglas Ferguson to inform you of the implications of this insanity, and the ramifications impacting upon the whole issue of indigenous survival. But I will tell you they must be heard . . . They have shown a keen interest in connecting with the Hopis and other pueblo cultures of the U.S. Southwest.

Ali Sharif
Rainforest Information Centre, #504 G.
De Vargas Center
Santa Fe, New Mexico, USA

The basis of the indigenous struggle at the moment in Ecuador is the Indian Federations' project to have all indigenous land titled by 1992. This project is being coordinated on just about all geographic fronts and I personally believe that the fate of much of the existent rainforest in Ecuadorian oriente, some five million hectares, hangs in the balance.

Douglas Ferguson
Rainforest Information Center
344 A. Casilla
Ulloa y Ramirez Davilos
Sicursal 3, Quito, Ecuador

Our campaign needs to raise an average of 4-5 million signatures per month for the next 24 months. Can you help? . . . currently active through various networks in 70 countries worldwide, but getting a 'forest peoples' Charter' in place will take a lot of work and support.

Aubrey Meyer, Int'l Campaign Co-ordinator
SAVE THE FORESTS; SAVE THE PLANET
42 Windsor Road
London, NW2 5DS, United Kingdom

(September 1990 update: *A global referendum on the deforestation crisis! 3.3 million signatures already taken on a petition to the United Nations calling for an emergency debate in the General Assembly. 100 million signatures now sought worldwide by 1992. Support the World Rainforest Movement's "FOREST PEOPLES' CHARTER" based on the 'Penang Manifesto'.*)

Kristy Jane Norman: *I like trees because they absorb carbon dioxide. They give us paper and homes for birds.*

Chris Adams: *I want to tell you I like trees because they give us shade and food.*

Anonymous: *I went to the forest and I saw trees that were cut off in the middle. I saw trees that had stumps still.*

Daniel A. Smith: *We need to plant more and more trees every day because we're killing plants and animals and people.*

Amanda Folwell: *I heard we should replant trees so we can have shelter and food. Lots of people are cutting down too many trees. People could die without trees.*

Anonymous: *We need trees to build homes, but we need trees in the ground . . . because they stop the poison so we will not get sick. Besides, they make the woods. Trees are our friends.*

Niki Hamilton: *It is important that we replant trees so they will grow tall. We should take care of our resources so they will grow good and look pretty. They will look real pretty.*

Ms. Wilson's Class
Elliott Elementary
Irving, Texas, USA

Rainforest Information Center, Australia

Our classroom has been taking up loose change, competed in the Agricultural Youth Fair, and participated in other activities to raise money for the Children's Rain Forest in Costa Rica. We are buying back the forest at $50 per acre. We are now on our 15th acre!

> Norma S. Suddreth,
> Middle School Math/Science
> Lenoir, Nebraska, USA

(September 1990 update: *Now 27 acres saved.*)

This is to invite you to the next general meeting of the European Working Group on Amazonia to be held on January 19, 1990 in Brussels.

> European Environmental Bureau

We are coordinating efforts with several eco-groups in Austria and I'm going to Budapest next week to discuss a joint project with friends there. We have decided that donations for the day will go, via a local rainforest group, to the Penan tribe in Sarawak.

> Peter Schnitzler
> Vienna, Austria

As the monsoon rains have reached Burma, logging will be effectively stopped for several months. A number of the Thai logging companies have had great difficulty getting any wood out of their concessions due to the fighting; possibly some of these companies can be pressured into giving up the attempt. The US ban would certainly make a difference in that case, and might save whole pockets of forest in some of the more "difficult" concession areas.

> Edith T. Mirante
> Project Maje
> 14 Dartmouth Road
> Cranford, New Jersey, USA

Dear People,
        I would like to plant trees. Do you know were I can begin at. I live in Altoona, Pennsylvania. I planted a pine tree it is still alive. I really want to get rid of pollution. I don't think it is right to cut down trees. Can you give me all the materials and information I need. When I grow up I want to be a person who plants trees.

        Thanks.

        your freind

        Kimberly Stein

P.S I don't know what place I can plant trees and do I need seeds.
        My adress is 51 150th St, Altoona, PA. 16602.

18 May 1990
GK-KK/90-814

Mr. Mark Dubois
International Coordinator
Earth Day 1990
P.O. Box AA
Stanford University
California 94309
U.S.A.

Dear Mr. Dubois,

Thank you for your letter of 20 April and the April Update.

The Green November was formed in November 1989 when 32 Burmese met
at a training called 'Leadership Formation Programme for Burma'.
We have in our group Burma's ethnic nationals such as, Arakan,
Burman, Kachin, Karen, Karenni, Lahu, Mon, Pa-Oh, Shan and Wa.
We have medical doctors, lawyers, educationists, students and one
Buddhist monk.

Our main aims and objectives are the preservation of our country's
enviroments, preservation of indigenous rights, t he restoration
of democracy and human rights in Burma.

We were not able to celebrate Earth Day 1990, except our issuing a
Green November 32 post-card with a slogan 'Peaceful Green World'.
The reason that we were not able to celebrate the Earth Day 1990
was that we were occupied defending our forests from the invasion
of Rangoon military junta troops. One of our members, Dr. Min
Thein, an ethnic Burman, was captured by the Rangoon troops and
beheaded. He died defending mother nature.

Sincerely yours,

Em Marta

Em Marta, Secretary
The Democratic Alliance of Burma
P.O. Box 11-792
Phrakhanong P.O.
Bankok 10110, Thailand

For our part, I would offer our farm to persons interested in knowing a lowlands rainforest environment, and experiencing life in a "buffer zone" where the forests are only beginning to shrink, where there is yet work to be done, and perhaps answers found before it is too late, and all wilderness pasteurized out of existence.

Meredith Foyle
Reserva Rio Guaycuyacu
Galapagos 565 #27
Quito, Ecuador

Anna Pilette
Monroe, Michigan, USA

4. There is no Sanctuary

Sometimes an incident is so emotional that newspapers, after exploiting the initial attention-getting headlines, cease thereafter to feature the story. We are left with only vague notions of what may be happening in the wake of incidents such as Bhopal, Chernobyl, and the Exxon Valdez. We may be curious, but we are, after all, far away from the actual gasping and dying.

But meanwhile, people do live under the clouds of these "accidents". Why, when one mountain lion attacks one child, do we send hoards of vigilantes to the mountains with guns, yet we accept a 20% increase in the cancer rate of our children with a sigh? We continue to drink from styrofoam cups even though (at the current rate of destruction) 20% of the earth's protective ozone will be gone in fifty years and a two hour exposure to the sun will result in blistered skin. Right now the hair of Russian children is falling out, yet we do not turn off our lights, turn down our thermostats, or ride the bus . . . but then, Russia is a long way off.

Earth Day 1990
Stanford University,
CA. 94309

Dear Earth Day 1990,
I am concerned about the Ozone Layer of our earth. If synthetic pollutants keep affecting the Ozone Layer the sun's ultraviolet rays will double almost triple in heat. I hope you understand what I am trying to say. If the earth's people don't do somthing now we won't ever be able to.

Thank you for your time.

Respectfully,

Lenny F. Galbicsek

Lenny F. Galbicsek
Brunswick, Ohio, USA

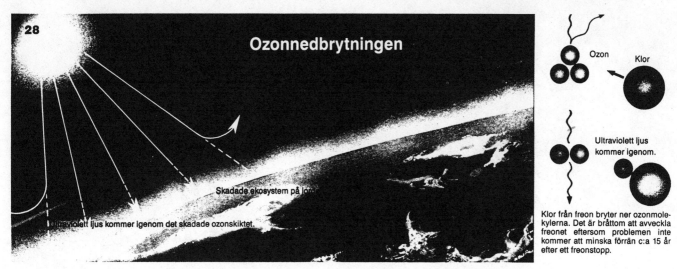

28

Ozonnedbrytningen

Ozon
Klor

Ultraviolett ljus kommer igenom.

Skadade ekosystem på jorden

Ultraviolett ljus kommer igenom det skadade ozonskiktet.

Klor från freon bryter ner ozonmolekylerna. Det är bråttom att avveckla freonet eftersom problemen inte kommer att minska förrän c:a 15 år efter ett freonstopp.

Jenny Ljungqvst
ISU AB, Sweden

I would like to talk to you about the world. It concerns me a lot. Little by little the world is disappearing, by pollution, litter, toxic waste. What will happen to us? Our future is very dark. Especially for little kids when they grow up. Their kids are going to wish they were us so they could have seen the world in one piece or if the world is still there.

Lacey Dudas
8164 North Akins
North Royalton, Ohio, USA

I'd like to drive down the street with my windows rolled down and not choke on the fumes from buses and big trucks. What can I do to help in controlling the major smog problem we have here in the San Fernando Valley and all over the world?

Jennifer L. Wales
West Hills, California, USA

. Motorists in the southland waste 3 million (of the 12 million gallons of fuel burned every day in the region) while idling in traffic jams . . . The wasted fuel is directly converted to air pollution. Overall . . . traffic congestion in the southland costs motorists some $9.4 billion a year . . .

USA

Frantisek Jablonovsky
Czechoslovakia

I am an American citizen living in Santiago, Chile--an unbelievably polluted place . . .

Kathryn Mickle
Galvarino Gallardo 2086 #32, Santiago, Chile

I don't know if you've ever been to Bangkok, but our air is unbelievable - buses, cars, and motorcycles belching black smoke all day and most of the night. His Majesty says that if the water isn't cleaned up and something concrete done about pollution, within ten years no one will be able to live in Bangkok. Pretty scary, yet people still don't take the situation seriously.

Mrs. Bonnie Davis
Bangkok, Thailand

I'm 13 years old and have . . . watched the hot, smoggy, muggy days turn into cloudy, cold, rainy days . . . The very next day the once blue skies are yellow-grey from smog.
Sometimes I feel so helpless about stopping world problems, I cry.

Maya Hagege
6615 Burnet Avenue
Van Nuys, California, USA

To whom it may concern:

My name is Sean Taylor and I am very concerned about our enviroment. I go hunting with my dad and sometimes I wonder how long these woods will last. We fish too, but we can't fish at our favorite river anymore.

I would appreciate if you would send me some information about Earth Day and how I can help clean up the enviroment.

Sincerely,
Sean Taylor

Sean Taylor
364 S. Harrison
Kirkwood, Missouri, USA

Hi, my name is Kristen Carreras. I am very concerned about the environment. For years I watched incinerators burn garbage and pollute the atmosphere. I've seen the forest next to my house slowly come down . . . and I am shocked about the destruction of the rainforest. What can I do?

Kristen Carreras
New Bedford, Massachusetts, USA

Despite a Mediterranean Action Plan of the U.N. since 1975, and various treaties, the Med is the world's dirtiest sea, heading for mega-eco catastrophe because of exploding population growth in south and east, ditto of tourists, and runaway deterioration of already pretty bad problems such as waste disposal, water supplies, erosion, pollution of sea and rivers . . . all made much worse by climate change.

Vanya Walker-Leigh
Gibraltar

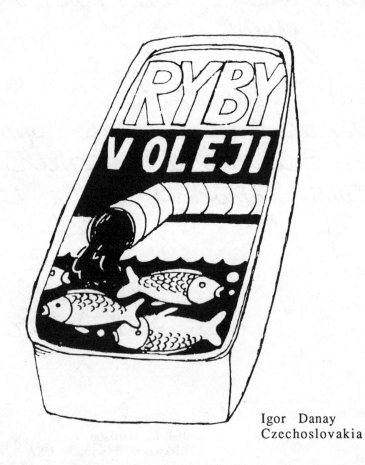

Igor Danay
Czechoslovakia

The mountains of Europe are part of the cryosphere, the ice and snow regions of the earth. The cryosphere plays an important part in determining the climate. Ice sheets reflect back insolation (albedo effect) and hence lower temperatures. Glaciers and underground permafrost melt to provide sources of the great rivers of Europe which irrigate the plains, provide water for cities and factories, and barges to the seas.

Since the middle of the 19th Century, the glaciers have been retreating and this trend has been accentuated in recent years, with higher temperatures and less snow to feed them. Now the Alpine glaciers are only 70% of their 1850 extent and the Rhine glaciers have lost 50%.

ALP ACTION
Switzerland

Whenever I look around my neighborhood, my school, or even the parks I see litter and pollution. Every day I see people throwing trash on the ground without a second thought. I see people killing plants, and breaking branches off trees. These problems exist in my school alone. The problems that our country faces are even greater.

USA

When we were young, the streams and the springs in Kumamoto were clean and pure. They abounded with all forms of life: water-beetles, water-spiders and water-boatmen among many others. The river banks were carpeted with flowers in Spring. Things have changed. Children today do not know, have not once seen, these creatures, and furthermore, they have never even swum in the rivers. In many places, it is not safe to drink the spring water any more. In the past thirty years or so, our natural environment has degenerated.

Looking at today's world, it is plain to see that culture and civilization, as well as the crisis that we face, transcend national boundaries. The destruction of the world's tropical rain forests has begun to severely disturb the planet's meteorological balance. Abnormal amounts of radioactivity, originating from the Chernobyl nuclear accident, were measured even here in Kyushu. We daily consume radioactively contaminated foodstuffs . . .

The Kumamoto Earth Day Committee
YMCA International Center
12-24 Hanabata Cho, 860 Kumamoto Shi
Japan

Dick Holst
ISU AB, Sweden

As I wrote earlier, Earth Day 1990 in the Ukraine will be the opening day of Chernobyl Week. We propose for April 22: 1) Stop the traffic (except electric) in the central parts of cities, 2) Hold rallies and demonstrations especially near sources of environmental contamination. On April 24-25 an international conference on pro-radiological, medical, and social problems arising from Chernobyl disaster.

We proposed to declare April 26 as the day of national mourning, and recently this proposal was adopted by the Supreme Soviet of the Ukraine. Special services are proposed to be carried out on the central squares of cities (beginning at 6:00 pm) all over the Ukraine. At 8:00 pm, ten minutes of national mourning (will begin): traffic is stopped; bells are ringing; candles are burning. At 10:00 pm, turning off lights in flats; candles remain burning.

Andriy Demydenko, Ukranian Environmental Association, Zeleny Svit (Green World)
5a Kirow Street
252021 Kiyev, Ukraine, (USSR)

The fallout from the Chernobyl accident in April, 1986 came as a rude shock to Italians who never imagined that an explosion so far away could affect them. Parts of northern Italy suffered considerable contamination by radioactive iodine and cesium, requiring people to avoid milk and certain vegetables for several months.

World Watch
July/August 1989

Geneva (AP) - A member of the Soviet Parliament said Thursday that about $320 billion will be needed to cope with the consequences of the Chernobyl nuclear disaster during the next 10 years.

Yuri Shtsherbak, vice chairman of the Supreme Soviet's Commission on Environment and Nuclear Energy . . . said almost 4 million people are still living in regions with higher than normal levels of radiation. The accident occurred April 26, 1986.

Reprinted with permission of
The Associated Press in
The Anchorage Times
Anchorage, Alaska, USA

FOR IMMEDIATE RELEASE

Press Release
6 April 1990

ANCHORAGE, Alaska --- When Tom McDowell recently returned from his second trip to the Soviet Union, he knew he had to act on what he had whitnessed. McDowell, a professional videographer, visited the city (and surrounding area) that had been Chernobyl. He recorded numerous former residents and officials -- all willing to talk not just about the horrible devastation of the reactor meltdown of four years ago, but eager to discuss what is happening in the aftermath of the disaster.

McDowell was contacted, while in the Soviet Union, by an organization called UNION CHERNOBYL U.S.S.R. He discovered the ongoing suffering of over 5 million Soviets who live near the disaster zone. He was introduced to doctors, nurses, teachers, and many others who are working hard at trying to meet the challenges of dealing with the many and varied medical problems associated with radiation exposure. And then he saw the children. At one location . . . school classes had been set up to try to deal with the special needs of children who are suffering from at least six different blood diseases . . . He asked what he could do. The reply from officials of UNION CHERNOBYL U.S.S.R. was direct: Help us set up a UNION CHERNOBYL USA that could help the the people of North America begin to understand that we have very serious problems here in Kiev and the areas surrounding Chernobyl. Help them understand we need medical supplies . . . let them know we need humanitarian assistance.

UNION CHERNOBYL USA/I CARE
1013 East Diamond Boulevard, Suite 601
Anchorage, Alaska, USA

Why should the European community turn its attention to Lithuania, the Baltic republic that is no different environmentally from other economically-stagnant nations where staggering amounts of industrial waste slip past rudimentary pollution controls, and regulations--if extant--are easily ignored . . . ?

Because Lithuania also has the Ignalina nuclear power plant, which environmentalists and scientists argue is a second Chernobyl waiting to happen.

Designed to be the largest nuclear plant in the USSR, Ignalina is the largest virtual clone of the Chernobyl plant using the same outdated RMBX reactors that are prone to explosions. Under total manual operation, these reactors allow staff (only) one minute to respond before a problem becomes critical.

Worse, Ignalina appears to have been built on or near a tectonic fault . . . Fires and various accidents occur frequently, construction quality is poor, and radiation emissions are (very likely) contaminating the entire country's well water supply.

If an accident were to occur at Ignalina, like Chernobyl its catastrophic radioactive impact would be felt all over Europe for years to come.

Lithuania

If we continue to act as though there were no tomorrow, there could be no tomorrow.

Jamaica

Jan Kolla
Czechoslovakia

بسم الله الرحمن الرحيم

ATTORNEY–GENERAL
Male'
Republic of Maldives

Madam,

The Republic of Maldives comprise some 1200 small
low-lying coral islands in the Indian Ocean some 420 miles south-
west of Sri Lanka. Naturally divided into groups of islands
called " atolls " the Maldives are spread out in a double chain
over an area about 500 miles x about 76 miles of the Indian
Ocean.

There are no mountains or forests. Coconut palms
and thickets of tropical under growth are the main natural
vegetation. None of the islands are more than 7 feet above sea-
level, and nature has given us security by a barrier reef that
runs almost totally around the archipelago.

I do not know whether you have heard of our small
country with just over 200,000 population. Hence the above very
brief discription to show you how much we would concern ourselves
with the continuous changes in the weather pattern the world over
and also the sea rise about which numerous international conferences,
seminars and other meetings have been held.

Yours Sincerely

Ahmed Zaki
Attorney-General

I've heard the ocean will rise 16 feet in the next forty years. Thus destroying valuable seaside properties throughout the world.

Jonathan Collyer
Los Gatos, California, USA

What concerns me the most is what will happen to us when the earth comes to an end? I'm very worried about this! Thank you for your time.

Leslie Filipow
North Royalton, Ohio, USA

I am a young student in the state of Louisiana who has the same dreams as many other people my age. I hope to be able to live in this same world in years to come. EACH year, EACH day, EACH minute that goes by, I know that my planet is being destroyed, and I wish I could help to stop, or at least slow down, the process.

Viki Lyne Armentor
Sunset, Louisiana, USA

I think that most people are aware that we are murdering our earth. The problem encompasses so many aspects of our society that we may be over-whelmed to the point of resignation.

Shirley Tovar-Allen
624 S. Sibley Street
Buckner, Missouri, USA

Vladimir Pavlik
Czechoslovakia

Dear Earth Day Folks   2/26/89
    Greetings from Alaska.
    In 1972 I left my Porsche and house-
boat bachelor pad in the San Francisco
Bay area, and moved to Sadie Cove,
Alaska. My desire to live a simpler
cleaner life surrounded by nature called
me north, and over the past eighteen
years I've built my home and lodge
where the mountains meet the sea.
Over the years I've been involved in
local environmental issues, but had
a philosophy of—let the rest of the
world live in their own waste and
pollution. Then last year the Exxon
Valdez fouled my front yard with 11
million gallons of black death. After
working on the oil spill clean-up
for 4 1/2 months I realized there is
no sanctuary

                    My best,
                    Keith Iverson

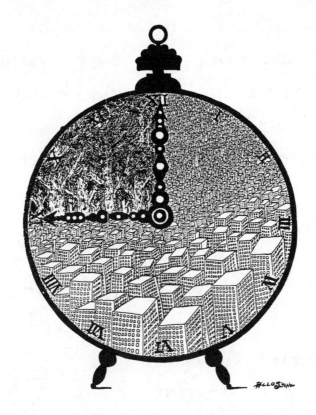

Jeno Dallos
Uj Ludas Mgz., Hungary

5. HOW MANY?

He goes out to the garden where his seed flats sit on a black table, tilted toward the winter sun. A handful of sprouts already touch and sweat against the covering glass. Dark green and healthy, their leaves overlap, casting shadows, claiming space.

He wants his garden to have diversity, health and productivity, so he has divided his garden plot to give each plant enough air, light, nutrients and water. His plan calls for five tomato plants. He planted twelve tomato seeds. Nine sprouted. In the black soil their roots already intertwine and compete. Soon the plants will be root-bound; growth will stop. Even now, in order to transplant them, their roots will have to be torn apart. It is time to thin the vegetables. He takes four from the warm bed and tosses them on the compost heap. The five survivors will do well. He knows that is how it is done, how a gardener does it. He knows that if the gardener does not do it, the plants do it to themselves; they will be unhealthy and stunted, and he will have fewer tomatoes. Emotionally, it is not easy for him to thin the vegetables, and so each season he plants fewer seeds.

HELLO -

I'm writing to let you know I agree with earth day and read Earth Day 1990.

It's a lesson plan and Home Survey booklet.

What bothers me is only one thing - if we are trying to keep the earth clean, etc. Why can't Babies be part of the earth day?

It's people isn't it? I know its a hard subject - but if you want to save the earth - how about saving babies. Well - you know where I stand on Abortion now. I don't plan to make a big thing out of it - I'm just curious and won't be causing any problems. I just need an answer.

Respectfully -
Mrs. Betty Creager

Mrs. Betty Creager
Greenville, South Carolina, USA

I would be very happy to participate in what may be the most important environmental event of the century. Wein-Surat city has about 2 million population and faces a most serious problem in the slums. About 0.8 million people rot in the slums. They have no good houses, (only) shanty huts, most dirty water, unhygienic conditions, over population. Worst of these things is about 0.4 million ladies have no latrines so they cannot reply to the call of nature easily, hence, they cannot cover their shame.

India

Hello--sorry no $. I support other groups doing Earth-help projects.
With your global roster of sponsors and international scope, where oh where is the

OVER
POPULATION
PROBLEM
???

Someone has to start to talk about it. I wish it was you.

USA

I had already made out my check, and then I came to your agenda's part of Family Planning "stabilize world population." So you are lumping human life with nuclear waste, military expendings, etc. Let's kill babies and save trees! It's your mentality. Who are you to decide to kill babies? I don't give money to contribute to kill humans--unborn babies. "Planned" families is a cover up word for murder babies.

USA

As a vegan for many years I was glad to see your recommendation to eat lower on the food chain. In fact, all the Earth Day solutions were fine. I was, however, particularly interested to observe that one of the greatest contributions to earth pollution was never mentioned and that is OVER POPULATION. I realize this is a pretty touchy issue with many religious groups but it has to be faced. We are crowding all other life forms off the planet. Man's only enemy is himself. He dislikes discipline *in any form, and this is the one area he is loathe to address himself to. When and if you tabulate another list of earth day solutions, I hope you will mention this growing problem and approach it realistically.*

Edna L. Cowan
2701 3-Mile Run Road
Perkasie, Pennsylvania, USA

If "the one basic right of all species is the right to a future" . . . then shouldn't we all be Pro-Life? I believe that as protectors of the earth God gave us, we should also be committed to protecting human life. God creates every time conception occurs.

I know you didn't ask for a commentary on the abortion issue, but I feel strongly that many of our problems in this society (nationally and internationally) come down to TOLERANCE. We have tolerated for two decades the selfish, individualistic attitude that a woman has the right to do what she wants with her *body and government can't tell her not to kill her child, just as we have tolerated individuals and companies doing what they want to with their trash and their trees and BIG BUCKS have kept politicians from making the necessary changes to protect* LIFE *in both cases.*

Individualism gave us this pollution catastrophe!

Rhonda Brown
3101 N. Divis
Bethany, Oklahoma, USA

To Whom it May Concern:

I feel I can no longer support your efforts monitarily for a cleaner, healthier environment due to the amount of governmental lobbying that your environmental organizations are involved in.

I do not want my contribution dollars going for a lobbying effort for gun control, pro-choice, and other areas your groups promote.

I cannot in good faith support organizations that are involved with other organizations such as Planned Parenthood, National Education Association, Ted Turner & others that won't stand firm for traditional family values & strong morals.

Sincerely,
Tammi L. Sisk

RR1 Box 53
Antler, ND 58711

To this day the "Pro-Life" group is stronger than ever. They have the support of the President of the United States; also the United States Supreme Court . . . By the middle of the next century all the tropical rainforests will disappear: No forests; no oxygen; no life on planet earth!

Frank P. Meng
853 Jolanda Circle
Venice, Florida, USA

Make no mistake! I will not ever support post-conception (abortion) family planning! Show me that you are not killing children and I can support your efforts. Murder is not good for the earth. Please address this issue or my money will go to less drastic and more humane groups like The Nature Conservancy.

USA

I see no mention in your letter of population growth, population levels, or a population policy. Because population growth and accompanying industrialization to support increasing population levels are the cause of all our environmental problems, and because you don't refer to this cause, I cannot and will not be a "citizen sponsor of Earth Day."

Flora J. Spencer
2680 W., 33 N
Idaho Falls, Idaho, USA

Mo Udall is to be commended for his Earth Day solutions. However, all of these solutions are worthless if we do not deal with the primary cause of all environmental problems and that is overpopulation.

It is past time for us to face this issue and have population control or we are doomed. Life on earth, as we know it, cannot continue with the growing masses of humanity. We either have the wisdom to control our population or Mother Nature will, and nature is never kind!

E.E.S.
West Covina, California, USA

Dear Earth Day Officials,

I've seen the list of 110 things you can do to save the planet and I think that instead you should tell people that the #1 thing they can do is have fewer kids.

We have limited land and resources and thus we must have a limited population! In 1930 we had 2 billion people, now we have 5 and even if the growth rate stays the same and does not increase we will have 8 billion in another 30 years!

If we continue as we are, we will reach our limits soon and have massive hunger and wars, competing for the scarce resources. Why wait until then when we can do something now?

While recycling and putting bricks in the toilets will delay the crisis, the real answer is:

NEGATIVE POPULATION GROWTH!

Sincerely,

Nicole Schmid
San Carlos, California, USA

International Society of Naturalists

[Founder President : The Late Lt. Col. Fatehsinghrao P. Gaekwad]

C/o. Maharaja Fatehsingh Zoo Trust,
Indumati Mahal,
Jawaharlal Nehru Marg,
BARODA 390 001. INDIA
[Telegrams : INSONA]

For correspondence write to:
Dr. G.M. Oza, INSONA,
Oza Building, Salatwada,
Baroda - 390 001, INDIA

May 1990

Global Population Problems & Conservation Issues!

(Note presented by Conservationist Dr G M Oza from India, as a Panellist, in the Fourth International Conference on Environmental Future: Surviving With The Biosphere, held in Budapest, Hungary, 23- 27 April 1990.)

* * * * *

Can Man be prevented from destroying all life on Earth - including himself?

The obvious answer is that our first and foremost task is to control man's numbers, for he alone can be held responsible for endangering the future of mankind.

The most tragic aspect of the population explosion is that it is particularly in Asia, Africa and Latin America, where most of the people are already living at or near bear subsistence levels, with inadequate food, housing, education, and medical care, that the rates of growth are so alarmingly high.

Even in the underdeveloped countries which have adequate potential resources, excessive population growth is swamping agricultural economic development. The gap between the rich and poor nations is no longer merely a gap - it is a chasm. This is why the problem of population is an inseparable part of the larger overall problem of development and environmental maintenance.

Population growth must be controlled either by high death-rates or low birth-rates or by enlightened and artificial birth-control, accompanied by economic and social advancement, or by the ancient destroyers - pestilence, famine and war.

* * * * * * *

ENVIRONMENTAL
AWARENESS

Quarterly Journal
devoted to the cause of
Environmental Conservation
for Human Welfare.
Founding Editor : DR. G. M. OZA

President   *   Dr. (Smt.) Mrunalinidevi A. Puar
Vice-Presidents   *   Prof. T. Antony Davis, Shri Sangramsinh P. Gaekwad, Prof. R.N. Mehta
General Secretary *   Dr. G.M. Oza
Joint Secretaries *   Shri Satyajit S. Khachar, Smt. Premlata G. Oza
Treasurer   *   Dr. A.M. Parah

A LETTER TO 'EARTH DAY 1990'

We really should wake up to the fact that

it is not the Earth that needs saving.

The Earth could divest itself of man's noxious encrustations any time it desired. What needs saving is **mankind**, and from its own ignorance.

To repeat, mankind needs saving from **itself**, but the sheer weight and density of human ignorance persistently rules this out.

'Earth Day' literature is ultimately **trivial**, because it resolutely refuses to state

in plain words

the fact that mankind is breeding itself into a corner.

Unadulterated acknowledgement of human crassness is the sole key to healthy change; human beings continually fail to acknowledge the root: the insanity, stupidity and invalidity of

'Mother Right,'

that is, the assumed **'right'** of the female of this assumed species to reproduce! This **assumed right** is the key to all man's worries about the Earth.

Let us take good note that 'the Earth' doesn't need saving. The Earth doesn't even know about man!

As for man, that creature reached its cultural zenith a long time ago, and is now developing into

a monster of ignorance.

Raising money and hoo-ha for the mere concept of the Earth simply caters to man's vanity and diverts attention from the heart of the problem.

USA

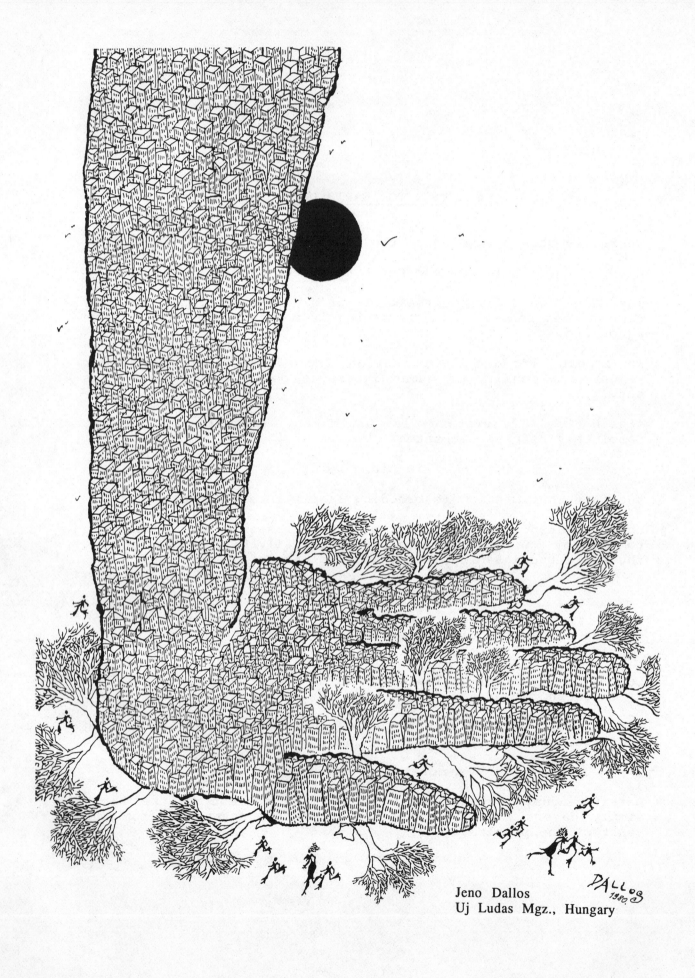

Jeno Dallos
Uj Ludas Mgz., Hungary

March 13, 1990

Dear Earth Day 1990 organizers,

Your agenda for Earth Day 1990 is noble; however, it is blatantly missing <u>one</u> essential in "specific accomplishments". Of your 1 to 10 where oh where is population control & reduction? That should be priority #1. I say this as a right-wing Republican. If someone as conservative as myself sees this as necessary to implement your hoped "accomplishments", don't you think that the majority of the less conservative population would wonder how you missed the issue? Don't be so squimish!

Very sincerely,

Virginia I. Pisias

P.S.
I'm also anti-abortion and have 3 children. <u>Still</u> I see population control, hopefully through education, as necessary for survival.

Virginia I. Pisias
San Francisco, California, USA

Peter Kuliffay
Czechoslovakia

6. Econology

All pollutions are caused by the production, use, and disposal of things. If we drove no cars, we would have no global warming. If we used no CFC's to make styrofoam cups, refrigerators, air conditioners, or computers and chips, then we would have no worries about ozone depletion. If we made no chemical fertilizers, pesticides, and herbicides, our soil and ground water would not be contaminated . . . and we would have fewer cancers. Things: houses full of things; garages full of things; storage facilities full of things. And they all have taken energy to produce, they take energy to keep or to run, and at some time they will have to be disposed of.

Never will we stop buying and using things. But we can let our money work for a better environment by buying more consciously. Ultimately, the person responsible for cutting down the forest is not the logger who needs the job but the consumer who buys the forest products: the wood, the beef, or the unrecycled paper.

We might also ask ourselves why we are willing to pay the chairman of an automobile manufacturing company $10 million a year, and only one one-hundredth of that amount to the United States Secretary of Education. Is a good democracy based on the quality of cars we produce or on the quality of people we fashion in our schools?

Support for Earth Day came from institutions throughout our society, from the UAW and the Department of Defense, as well as from inside and outside of corporations. Although many individuals were critical of corporate greed, irresponsible methods of production, and poisonous products, others pointed out that if we did not demand gasoline, Exxon would not be shipping oil around. Many corporations encouraged Earth Day and promoted environmental consciousness with their employees. General Dynamics, for example, printed (on recycled paper with lead-free, low VOC inks) a pamphlet with detailed instructions on how one can plant a tree. Included was a story about how their engineers discovered and changed the lighting at Cape Canaveral (which had been disorienting the baby sea turtles trying to find the sea), and with information on how department heads are using innovation to reduce waste and CFC's.

Many believe that to choose a healthy ecology is to choose against a healthy economy. Yet, much of our environment is lost due to a lack or shortage of funds. As soon as we are able to see that all sides are concerned, that all sides are responsible, and that all sides need to act, then perhaps we will discover that a solution to the environmental crisis lies not *in* the conflict of ecology versus economy, but *beyond* the conflict: econology.

(All letters came to us unsolicited. Products and claims have not been examined.)

You are probably aware of the desperate socio-economic condition prevailing in Bangladesh caused by excessive unemployment, extremely poor planning, and a continuously deteriorating law-and-order situation which has left little or no time for the common masses to participate in such urgent activities as Earth Day.

Md Mozammel Haque, Director
United Club, GPO Box 2296
Dhaka-1000, Bangladesh

I am increasingly bothered by the way we have a tendency to destroy all that is innocent and beautiful. Man will do just about anything for money. I feel like I am helpless in an attempt to end all this. I know it will probably never be totally possible, but I'll never give up. I've tried recycling, picking up trash, and other stuff, but it just isn't enough. I'm only 16 but I want to help out all I can. Why would someone want to slaughter a whale just for the shampoo?

Joe David Pena
Florence, Mississippi, USA

A lot of mining is done in my country - Bauxite, Rutile, Iron Ore, Diamonds, and Gold. A large portion of our land has been destroyed and the mining companies have done nothing to reclaim it for food production.

United Nations of Youth
G.P.O. Siaka Stevens Street
Freetown, Sierra Leone, West Africa

Mahatma Gandhiji was one of the earliest leaders who foresaw the evil effects of centralized industrialism and materialism causing serious havoc on Nature as well as on the poor masses of people. "Mother Nature has enough to meet the needs of all men, but not to cater to the greed of Man" was his famous saying

India

The teachers and students of our school are . . . worried at the serious ecological problems in the world and particularly in our native town of Cherkassy. It is known as the town of "big chemistry" and we are aware that it leads to a lot of troubles. . . Many people of our region . . . show their real concern about the harmful level of air and water pollution and injurious industrial wastes in our town.

K. Kirillova & L. Pobyvanets
School No 1,
Cherkassy, USSR

At the age of 17, I was diagnosed as having environmental illness. I received treatment from the Environmental Health Center in Dallas, Texas. I was much better until I was chemically poisoned at my job at a PBS station in Buffalo . . . When I am healthy again, I want to dedicate my entire life to improving the environment. I lived very close to Niagara Falls, which created my environmental illness in the first place.

USA

. . . we are the little polluters and wasters. The biggies are the power and money people.

Before this nation was developed, it was rich in natural resources. Then came the needy and greedy, conquering and destroying the land and water. Common sense was forgotten when industry was introduced.

We reap what we sow, and this coveted land of rich soil, fresh water, and beauty was converted into ugliness. Now we have garbage, fumes, polluted water, naked forests, haze, etc.

Science fools us into believing that Mankind is better than ever, but the truth is we humans are becoming weaker, and the environment worse.

M. Fankhauser
403 Adelaide Street
Minerva, Ohio, USA

It's about time people started <u>giving</u> back to the Earth Mother, instead of just take, take, taking all the time!

Lorraine Marie Fisher "Gypsy"
5829 Hosac Way
Citrus Heights, California, USA

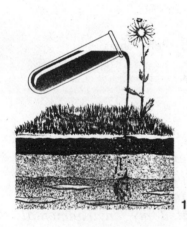

1960   1980   2000

Dick Holst
ISU AB, Sweden

Earth Day 1990
P.O. Box AA
Stanford University
California 94305
(415) 321-1990

To whom it may concern,

    The main purpose of this letter is to ask for as much information as possible about "Earth Day 1990." I would also ask that any information about past Earth Days, especially Earth Day 1970, could be sent for publicity reasons.
    I would like to mention why we, the Niagara University Student Government Environmental Committee, want to get involved in Earth Day 1990. Niagara University is situated about 200 yards from the Hyde Park Landfill, a former Hooker Chemical site, a few miles from such chemical companies as Occidental, DuPont, and Olin located on the Niagara River, a few minutes from Love Canal, and minutes from the "Green Mountain" of CECOS International.
    The committee I chair, consisting of 20 active student members, has been attending various meetings around our area and also around New York State. We collect information and relay it to our fellow students through such manners as environmental committee meetings, student government meetings, and the student newspaper, the Niagara Index.
    I, personally, would like to see this be a big event held on the campus of Niagara University. This brings me to a large problem, the administration. Our university is heavily supported, financially, by the chemical companies of the area. The smallest mention of the environment sparks problems.
    I believe if the committee I head handles this correctly in conjunction with our university, other area colleges, community groups, local businesses, and you, it can be a hugh success. We have pushed the barrier away a small amount, but this could open the doors for communication between the students and the environment, but I need your help.
    I would also ask that you send any contacts you believe would help us, and any ideas that you might have for us. It would be much appreciated.

                    Sincerely,

                    Timothy A. Gabel
                    Chairperson

                            Timothy A. Gabel
                            NUSG Environmental Committee
                            Niagara, New York, USA

P.O. Box 2163
Lenox, MA 01240-5163

Christina Desser
Earth Day
504 Emerson Street
Palo Alto, CA 94301

April 6, 1990

Dear Ms. Desser:

I wanted to talk with you because I understand that your organization has made it a policy not to accept any chemical company as a sponsor. I work for the plastics division of a large corporation; we are essentially a chemical company. However, my company is working closely with local organizers of Earth Day to educate people on how to dispose of household wastes. You see, our company has a strong commitment to protecting the environment, including emissions reduction and plastic recycling. We have made investments in plant equipment and product-development programs which go way beyond what is required by law. I myself am a staunch environmentalist and I've seen my company work WITH environmentalists for a better, cleaner, more healthy world. Rather than making some blanket policy which pits you against ALL industrialists, you need to recognize that you have supporters within the "system" who can really achieve what you want to do.

Sincerely,

Robert Fireovid

Jozef Liptak
Czechoslovakia

Please let me know what I can do. I know for a fact that we are polluting our drinking water and the air we breathe. I used to be in the chemical industry in Texas.

Jean DeBlanc
Houston, Texas, USA

The company I work for, DuPont, is looking for ideas that the employees can participate in. I am also interested in events around the site. We are planning to celebrate not only Earth Day, but . . . Earth Week as well.

USA

I am writing to tell you what happens to people that try to help the environment.

In March 1985 I came up with an invention to cut back on toxic chemicals and waste for the pulp mills, so they would emit less pollution into our lakes and waterways. . . Kimberly Clark makes 118 fifty-ton cooks every 24 hours with their digestors. Bark drums don't remove all the bark, sand, or dirt from the logs. So I asked the operators about the amount of waste that goes through a digestor cook. A lot of this waste goes into our lakes as toxic waste . . . Using my invention to remove one ton or more of waste before each cook would allow the pulp mills to add a ton or more of good chips in its place per cook. The Kimberly Clark paper mill would make 118 tons more paper every 24 hours . . .

In 1986, I sent a letter to Mr. Vrooman of the Environment Ministry (about my invention). In January 1987, (he) was going to close the pulp mill because of the pollution laws they failed to obey. In February 1987, Mr. Vrooman was at (our local) high school to set the guidelines for the clean-up. I approached Mr. Vrooman and his people and gave them some more information in the form of a letter in front of the whole town. I asked him what he was going to do about the letter. He said he was leaving it up to Kimberly Clark.

Well, I found out what that meant. Two weeks later I was arrested on a Friday at about five o'clock just after work by the O.P.P. . . . They drove me to the jail. While this was going on with me, the O.P.P. raided my apartment and took all my papers, tapes, recorders, and books. . . (My invention) is what they were trying to steal. I was in jail for seven days and the Judges made me stay in Thunder Bay for thirty days more. . .

Mr. Vrooman quit the Ministry shortly after my trial and started working for Great Lakes Paper, Ltd.

Gary Crozier
Box 1368, Station B
Weston, Ontario
M9L 2W9, Canada

I'm also interested in a list of companies that are good to the environment and those that are negligent so that I can make my money speak for me when I'm choosing a product. And you can bet I'll pass the word along about which company to buy from and which one not to.

Teresa McCartney
Kirksville, Missouri, USA

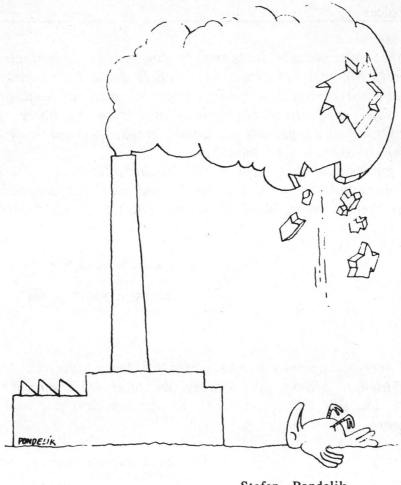

Stefan Pondelik
Czechslovakia

On EcoNet (an environmental computer network) people, using their personal computers, sent information to each other over regular telephone lines. The democratic and egalitarian nature of computer telecommunications was demonstrated by the wide range of perspectives voiced about such issues as whether Earth Day should accept money from a corporation with a questionable environmental record . . .

The messages came from Leningrad and Mexico City, from Alaska and Florida, from London and Taiwan. And the central Earth Day office communicated with their regional offices throughout the world . . . and all this without using a single tree!

Bill Leland
Director, EcoNet
3118 Sacramento Street
San Francisco, California, USA
Telex: 154205417

As Americans have become increasingly concerned about their exposure to pesticides, especially for their children, researchers have been working to develop environmentally safe alternatives. A wide variety of methods and products are now available to safely and effectively control insects in the home. These include citrus extracts, insecticidal soaps, sex attractant traps, diatomaceous earth, boric acid, insect growth hormones, and many others.

A resource guide, available from Earth Stewardship Press, provides a list of suppliers of environmentally safe pest control products, and sources of information on safe pest control in the home. Send $1.00 and SASE to "Safe Pest Control Resource Guide."

Earth Stewardship Press
Box 1316
Sterling, Virginia, USA

We are the largest company in the world for the production of beneficial insects which are used to combat pest insects. We offer more than 55 biologicals as well as plant care and soil management. All of our products are non-toxic, non-polluting, and organic.

Sheri Herrera de Frey, V.P.
ARBICO, Inc.
Environmental Alternatives
Tucson, Arizona, USA

. . . Louis O. Werneke Company . . . is a pioneer in the manufacture and distribution of Solvent Safe inks, a water base product which is approved in writing by the USDA and accepted by the FDA.

As you probably know, printing inks in general use chemical solvents as a base, and are therefore a large generator of hazardous wastes. Solvent Safe inks have been acclaimed by the Minnesota State Waste Management Board and other groups who know that the safest, most lasting solution for managing hazardous waste lies in reducing waste at its source.

William J. Hanvik
Ad Copy Services, Inc.
5520 Upton Avenue South
Minneapolis, Minnesotta, USA

Our land fills are all but filled and are causing more hazards to our earth than most other environmental problems around, yet not enough people realize what's available on the market.

I have been an avid believer in environmental issues for most of my life, so much so that I took employment with Pan American Resources, Inc. a company that is involved in manufacturing waste distillators. The waste distillator is a non-burning process that turns solid waste into char, while emitting very little if any emissions into the environment.

Thomas R. Wiley Jr.
Pan American Resources, Inc.
1656 West 9th Street, Bldg. C
Upland, California, USA

I am in the process of trying to put together a recycling program with my company and, needless to say, I have found many obstacles. Mainly the fact that it may cost several hundred dollars to get this project started, and also it will not necessarily generate a lot of money. I am very interested in learning more about what I can do to help persuade upper management in my company to understand the importance of recycling, and purchasing recycled paper.

I work for a bank and 95% of our waste is white paper.

Laina P. Maxwell
Lithonia, Georgia, USA

I wanted to be sure that you are aware of our unique program, Why Waste a Second Chance? a small town guide to recycling.

Since its release last year, Why Waste a Second Chance? *has been used by hundreds of small towns, community groups, neighborhood organizations, religious groups, clubs, agencies, and others to begin successful recycling programs.*
Why Waste a Second Chance? offers a wealth of information, advice, and ideas that communities can use as the basis for an effective recycling project, tailored to meet their own needs.

Bruce G. Rosenthal
National Assn. of Towns and Townships
1522 K Street, N.W. Suite 730
Washington, DC, USA

RECYCLE.

Avoid Extinction.

Phil Yeh
Cartoonists Across America
Lompoc, California, USA

As an American Airlines Flight Attendant I am part of a recycling project at my home base in Nashville, TN. Our west coast bases have sucessfully recycled soda cans and newspaper from the airplanes as they come in to the airports in San Jose, San Francisco, San Diego and L.A. Nashville will be kicking off our recycling efforts at the airport Flight Service operations area on Fri., April 20, in recognition of Earth Day on the 22nd. Any information you could send me would be much appreciated. We would like very much to be a part of the celebration!

Sincerely,

Toni Simpson

Toni L. Simpson
Nashville, Tennessee, USA

ALP ACTION : The Concept

1. ALP ACTION is a new framework for environmental action for the corporate community.

2. It intends to bring about a total switch with respect to the present situation : the corporate sector is seen to be largely responsible for the threat to ecosystems - we wish to show that businesses can become responsible for their preservation. The future is in the hands of the private sector - we must provide the means for it to contribute to environmental protection.

3. ALP ACTION will become a system within which business becomes the guarantor and, indeed, the leader of individual projects which collectively contribute to the protection of the Alpine environment based on sustainable development.

4. To achieve this, we recognize that business in general has long-term goals. The protection of the environment is a long-term necessity. Who, today, is better equipped than the corporate sector to take on the challenge of efficient management of natural resources ? It is the management of these resources that the world urgently needs.

5. What is lacking is opportunity : the majority of firms do not have the means nor the knowledge required to initiate or assess programmes for environmental protection. Besides, such programmes are not currently on their list of priorities. Through information and careful evaluation, we know that most firms will support programmes to safeguard nature if these are (i) not in conflict with their interests, (ii) reliable in terms of their effectiveness, and (iii) devoid of socio-political controversy.

6. Such projects exist. ALP ACTION has identified several. We shall continue selecting the most immediately effective, sustainable, and useful projects and bring them to the attention of individual companies which are most likely to be interested in investing in them. ALP ACTION provides technical and scientific data to help company executives to choose projects for sponsoring. This introduces the information and educational aspect which is crucial to the programme's long-term success.

7. ALP ACTION offers a moral and scientific guarantee to investors for the success of the projects it proposes. The whole ALP ACTION programme is based upon exclusivity, i.e. one project - one company. Incentives such as the enhancement of corporate image and product publicity are crucial to achieve success. Therefore, we will seek and negociate various kinds of agreements with project managers, local authorities, regional, national and international media in order to make sure that the investing companies get their deserved share of credit for their project's success.

8. Our role is also to monitor the results of these projects in order to steadily build-up our knowledge-base so that, with time, companies will be able to predict precisely the returns on their investments in terms of benefits to their images and the promotion of their products and services.

Alp Action's first official corporate Sponsors are: Jacobs Suchard; Tetra Pak International, S.A.; Unigestion; Reuters S.A.; Republic National Bank of New York; Banque Bruxelles Lambert; Banque Pasche; Banque Paribas (Suisse) S.A.

MATTAWAN
Furnishings For The Home.

April 5, 1990

Mr. Denis Hayes
Chair and CEO
Earth Day 1990
P.O. Box AA
Stanford, California 94309

Dear Mr. Hayes:

I wanted to share with you this special edition poster which is our gift with every purchase in April. MATTAWAN has printed this commemorative poster to show our support for Earth Day and express our pledge to preserving the environment.

I believe that the 20th Anniversary of Earth Day on April 22 is the perfect opportunity to celebrate my store's decade-long commitment and tell others about the necessity of preserving the environment. MATTAWAN was conceived and has grown with this one premise in mind... to enhance the home lives of my customers with quality goods made from natural materials that do not endanger our world. I am proud that on this occasion, we can reaffirm this founding belief and share our commitment with others.

I wish to acknowledge the "pro-bono" services of the following individuals and companies who have contributed to 1% FOR EARTH:

Network Design Studio, Inc.   Lindenmeyr Munrow Paper Co.
Katie Kissane, Illustration   DOTS, Color Separations
Cross Pointe Paper Corp.   Ross Network, Printing

On May 1, I will present a check which represents 1% of MATTAWAN's April profits to Earth Day 1990/New York City. I commend this organization's efforts to make New York a more livable, environmentally aware city and I am proud to be a part of this project. Thank you for your editorial support of this important cause.

Sincerely,

Nancy Wykstra
Nancy Wykstra
President

(In March, one set of Earth Day environmental lesson plans, K-6 & 7-12, was sent free to each of the 80,000 schools in the United States. Teachers and all others had to buy their own copies. Some corporations, such as FERMI, were able to buy a couple of dozen sets.)

I feel your advertisement was misleading concerning your Earth Day 1990 curriculum. I felt that I would receive a kit for my classroom. Just because you have arranged for one curriculum (guide) to be distributed free to every school in the country doesn't necessarily mean that each teacher will get a chance to see it or use it. Sometimes materials are received and STORED. That doesn't help those teachers who are really concerned or interested. I spend a lot of money each year on my class. My feelings are hurt. We get no recompensation at all for anything extra we plan or do for our own classes. Some do NOTHING! Others do LITTLE! There are several who do EVERYTHING! ! !

Elaine T. Horlink, Ditson School, Grade 3
793 Boston Road
Billerica, Massachusetts, USA

Thank you for mailing this Earth Day 1990 material. I find it necessary to mail it back to you since at this time we do not have ten dollars ($10.00) in our budget. I had no idea there was a charge involved. Thank you.

Teacher
USA

This $12.00 was collected in my classes the week before school was out. The students would empty their pockets of pennies, nickles, and dimes each day. They set a goal of $10.00 and got $12.00. One student gave her lunch money for "her earth." It's a small amount but they were excited and it had to be counted daily. They were very proud of themselves!!

Patricia A. Malone
Chapman Middle School
Huntsville, Alabama, USA

"It will be a great day when our schools get all the money they need and the Air Force has to hold a bake sale to buy a bomber."

Istvan Krenner
Uj Ludas Mgz., Hungary

7. . . . for the people?

Politicians also helped the effort. Mo Udall sent out solicitations raising money for Earth Day. Many Members of Congress, as well as mayors and governors, were on the U.S. Board of Directors. Heads of State and U.N. officials joined the International Board. Throughout this last year, legislators nation-wide have introduced bills requiring recycling, cutting emission, and banning or restricting harmful products. Yet the letters we received consistently expressed frustration with politicians, and anger with a political system designed to promote compromise. On many of our current issues, compromise equals defeat. People seem to grasp the fact a little better than do their leaders that a species cannot be just a little extinct. As Democracy spreads around the globe, we might ask: Are these governments really ". . . of the people, by the people, and **for the people**"? Or is a more egalitarian form of government being hinted at in the writings of the world's people?

. . . we are going to organize regional membership of Earth Day in Taiwan. There are more than fifteen groups for environmental protection: grass-roots people, labor unions, woman's union, actors (actresses), students, communities . . . like to join this international movement.

Meanwhile, this is the first time, after 40 years of Marshall Law, (that) Taiwan citizen groups (are) joining international movement.

Taiwan

We are a small group of ecologs in Sabinov (East Slovakia) formed about a month ago, after the victory of democracy in our country. We are beginning modestly, without experience or means, only with a few followers because the force of totality exists still in our souls. Anyway, we have . . . pluck, and at the same time it's our human duty to rescue this planet.

Malecky Emil
Ruzova 08 301
Sabinov, Czechoslovakia

Excuse me for writing late! I think you surely know about our "Tender Revolution" . . . How marvelous! We obtain (from this) wider possibilities for Earth Day organizing, too.

Dr. Milan Kapusta
Slovak Union for Nature and Landscape
969 01 Banska.Stiavnica
Czechoslovakia

If the people of today do not get involved in our environment then it is just going to deteriorate and die. The people have to take a stand and let government officials know that they are not doing enough. And in the time it takes them to pass a bill, we, the people, could have already planted a forest.

Dominique Kantor
Birmingham, Alabama, USA

Gentlemen:

This morning there were eighteen doves and dozens of other birds (some so tiny that I had to smile and say a special prayer for the "least of these.") enjoying breakfast on the ground and from the feeders. Yes, we love the birds and all of God's precious creatures, especially the little dog we have, the fifth that someone has left on our porch. Our home is at the foot of a small mountain and we built here in order to enjoy the trees, etc. When the grosbeaks arrive, I feel like shouting for everyone to come and see them. The rabbits from the nearby hill enjoy the seed, also - "strange as it may seem!" We have always fed the birds and stray animals; but since our retirement, we have become real bird-watchers. We enjoy it!

Now...after building our home in Sunset and living here since 1953 (the sub-division is about 1/2 mile long and 150 people, mostly retired, live here), the W. Va. High-way Dept. has decided to put a 2-lane connector about 150 ft. from our home and 100 ft. above the connector will be a 4-lane highway with a median strip of 18 ft. Imagine! The Highway engineer tells us all trees will be cut down and a ground cover planted to hold the soil. A mansion and an adjoining pool slipped beyond repair on this same hill. The highway and connector will be a part of the ARC Corridor G (a federal project to help Appalachia). WE ARE DEVASTATED!

The Real Estate Division of the Highway Dept. said our homes would depreciate 50% in value (that I can't afford!), not to mention the horrors of the 2-year construction period, and then 15,000 cars, trucks, and coal transports running near our homes forever.

If anyone knows anything to do to help me, please call COLLECT (304) 235-2834. I have sought help from local, state, and federal sources (EPA says they go along with the states), but politicians are bedfellows and you can't win!

Sincerely,

Elizabeth Mottesheard

Elizabeth Moyer Mottesheard
42 North Sunset Boulevard
Williamson, West Virginia, USA

Community Health Foods

Making Natural & Organic Food Affordable

Dear Earth Day Members:

We live in a very beautiful area of northeastern Connecticut. However, I fear it will soon become more polluted than some of our surrounding cities. This is because our fearless leaders in Hartford are choosing incineration as a means to get rid of our hazardous wastes.

Just south of us a tire burning plant is beginning to be built in Sterling. In Preston, we will soon have a trash incinerator; and in our own town of Killingly, we are currently fighting a demolition wood burner.

After reading an article concerning your committee, it said that you would like to form an agency with authority to protect our atmosphere and our oceans. Well, all these plants are being pushed to be built before we have even begun to recycle! The people of our town are totally against these plants; however, it seems we don't have authority without our own communities anymore. That authority has been given up to commissions and agencies within Hartford.

I know the way they are going is the easy way out and the way out for a small group of people to make lots and lots of money. But it is not the healthiest way out for the majority of the people. If you should have any influence in anyway and have the authority to help us out, please do so before it is too late.

Very truly yours,

Linda D. Wojcik

Linda D. Wojcik
137 Green Hollow Road
Danielson, Connecticut, USA

To Anyone that can help,

Our town in Massachusetts is fighting a very frustrating fight, against our Politicians. The Massachusetts Water Resource Authority (MWRA) and the EPA have approved a sludge landfill in our town as part of the Boston Harbor cleanup. Our town is not against the harbor cleanup, but we are against the location of the landfill. Seven acres of this landfill is directly over our town's sole source aquifer. We believe this site was chosen because it is next to the state's only maximum security prison and the land is already state owned, cutting the cost of the cleanup. Cost should not be a factor. They'll only be spending more money, in the future, trying to clean our drinking water. Our town's aquifer supplies water to thousands of people in our town and neighboring towns. This aquifer feeds into the Stop River, which feeds into the Charles River and as you may know, runs into Boston. Therefore, the cleanup would start all over again. More money.

There is a second choice for this site on the Malden-Revere line, which the Boston newspapers have stated "is considered a "politically" unlikely choice since it is in House Speaker George Keverian's district." Even though it may be a safer site.

Our town and neighboring towns have had numerous demonstrations, written to many of our legislators, submitted our own test results and still, they won't listen. The MWRA's own test wells show that groundwater is within 6 feet of the surface over much of the site. All landfills leak. Our town is trying to save our water, which the Politicians in Boston don't seem to care about.

Right now we are fighting a bill that would transfer the land from the state to the MWRA. We have submitted our own bill to tranfer the land to the Corrections Department for construction of additional prison space, which is also desperately needed. Since our town houses the only maximum security prison in the state and has land for expansion, why not. No other town in the state has offered to house more or any prisons. I would hate to win this battle by way of prison expansion, but if that is what it takes, the people in our town are willing to do it.

Can You Please Help - Any Advice ????

A very concerned mother

Kathleen Cavanaugh

Kathleen Cavanaugh
Walpole, Massachusetts, USA

This letter is to notify all men and women running for office in the State of North Carolina that we will not vote for any person who has not shown some results in the war against pollution of our Planet Earth. We will not vote and we will endeavor to get others not to vote for persons who are afraid to pass (environment protection) bills . . .

For twenty years all of us have known what is happening to Planet Earth, but the problem has been ignored till now. Take a ride through western North Carolina and you can no longer ignore what is happening because you can see the dead trees standing like ghosts asking us the question: "Why? We have given you beauty, shade, provided your homes, your papers, protected the planet, and what did you (politicians) do? Cut us down! Trees which have been here for 100s of years, (you have) allowed pollution to poison us to the extent it kills us, and what are you (politicians) doing now that you see our ghosts standing in the forests? Nothing! . . . but there will come a day when your child will wander out and ask 'Where are the trees that we see in the books we read? Where are the animals? Where are the fish? Why do we have difficulty in breathing? Why do we suffer from extreme heat? Why didn't you do something?'" Yes, why didn't we?

Earl and Betty Wedge
237 Fulton Road
Franklin, North Carolina, USA

Vlado Javorsky
Czechoslovakia

A CONCURRENT RESOLUTION recognizing April 22, 1990 to be "Earth Day" in the Commonwealth of Kentucky.

"We do not inherit the earth from our parents, we borrow it from our children."

WHEREAS, almost twenty years ago, more than twenty million Americans joined together on Earth Day in a demonstration of concern for the environment; and

WHEREAS, this environmental even increased public awareness of the Earth's deterioration and resulted in the creation of new legislation protecting the Earth's air, water, and land; and

WHEREAS, despite environmental improvements, the health of the planet continues to be threatened by human activities; and

WHEREAS, Earth Day 1990 activities and events will educate citizens of the importance of acting in an environmentally sensitive fashion by recycling, conserving energy and water, using efficient transportation, and adopting more ecologically sound lifestyles; and

WHEREAS, Earth Day 1990 has more than a thousand affiliated organizations planning activities in more than 120 countries; and

WHEREAS, Earth Day 1990 is a call to action for all citizens to join in a global effort to better understand the planet in order to make wise decisions for the future;

NOW, THEREFORE,

Be it resolved by the House of Representatives of the General Assembly of the Commonwealth of Kentucky, the Senate concurring therein:

Section 1. That April 22, 1990, is recognized as "Earth Day" in the Commonwealth of Kentucky.

Section 2. That all state parks, state universities, and state agencies are encouraged to provide assistance in programs to improve environmental awareness and understanding of the planet.

Section 3. That all citizens of the Commonwealth of Kentucky are urged to join in a monumental, cooperative effort to look deeply at their own lives and ask whether their values, habits, and attitudes are compatible with the sustainable future we need to build.

Section 4. That copies of this resolution be transmitted to all Cabinet Secretaries and state universities of the Commonwealth of Kentucky, and to Earth Day 1990, P.O. Box AA, Stanford University, Stanford, California 94305.

Kentucky General Assembly
State Capitol Building
Frankfort, Kentucky, USA

In our country, ecological awareness and concern are almost unheard of . . . and governmental concern is only apparent.

Guatemala

Around the globe, today, the 22nd of April, people will observe world Earth Day. Over 100 nations spanning the six inhabited continents celebrate this day with activities that bring to fore the special, inviolate, yet often taken for granted relationship between Man and the Environment. I am, therefore, pleased to greet this gathering of earth savers

Our country observes world Earth Day amidst the compelling reality of environmental degradation. At this very moment, our country is threatened by the grip of the powerful El Nino, which may turn the current dry spell into a major drought. Already, the traditional rice granaries of western Visayas and central Luzon are suffering from lowered crop yields due to the lack of rainfall and the insufficiency of reservoirs and ground water.

Power outages have also become more frequent, due in part to the surge in power demand during the summer months, but more because of the decreased power output of our aging and heavily silted hydro-electric facilities.

In the midst of frequent brownouts, most of us say "Hindi, na baleng mawalan ng kuryente, huwag lang tubig." Yet, even the supply of water to the Metro Manila area is threatened by the dry spell. Since the early part of this year, the water levels of major reservoirs have been at critical levels and the extreme heat of the dry months have only served to accelerate evaporation. As we cast our sights for answers, we see not the light of hope, but the sight of denuded mountains and the signs of intense human activity in ecologically fragile uplands.

Obviously, the time of reckoning has come. We have exceeded the limits of Nature. Now, it is exacting its price.

Many ecological problems such as global warming, the destruction of the ozone layer and biodiversity pose challenges not just for us, Filipinos, but to all mankind. For one, the rate of destruction of our ozone layer--which shields mankind from, among others, cancer-causing ultra-violet rays--is alarming.

We in government, your administrators and legislators, are hard-pressed to come up with policies to meet these complex environmental problems. For policies must be in harmony with people's practices as well as tendencies.

President Corazon C. Aquino's Message for
Earth Day 1990
Kalayaan Studio, Malacanang
Philippines

SOS
Save Our Seafolks
Save Our Seas
Save Our Seanimals

HER EXCELLENCY
The President
Hon. Corazon Aquino

Dear President Aquino,

Happy Earth Day! We hope that your activities today will be very fruitful for saving our Mother Earth. Pollution has brought great havoc to our fishing grounds, and the same problems are being discussed over and over again yet their gravity has increased.

Yesterday, I, along with about 2,000 Earthsavers, was at the PICC having answered the call . . . to mobilize ourselves to save Mother Earth. Frankly, I am very disappointed in this meeting, a view which I am sure is shared by many participants. The reasons are very simple.

1. You did not come to address us personally. A great number of participants, especially the farm and sea folks, saw your absence as indicative of the weak "delagative" attitude and approach to the problem of the Environment. At the moment, closest to our hearts is a portion of Earth, the Philippines. We (and I suppose the rest of the world) wanted to hear what you will do to save our Motherland - ANG PILIPINAS.

2. This Earth Day meeting became the occasion where government distributed information of their agencies' programs and projects rather than AN OPPORTUNITY to gather feedback and people's suggestions so that such existing projects could be proceeding with greater vigor and better direction.

Government efforts to address our problems are perceived to be FRUSTRATING and too scattered. Two critical agencies vital to saving endangered Marinelife are presently on Staff Status. We are urging that you give them line-authority status, and that you transfer back to DENR all Fisheries Agencies so that pollution problems and productivity programs affecting the Marine and Aquatic sector could be addressed under one Department.

President Aquino, please give this matter your serious consideration.

Dante Par Pasia, President
Philippine Aquatic and Marinelife
(PARMACON)
P.O.Box 5037
Makati CPO, 1299 Philippines

I read today where scientists say that the Earth may become uninhabitable in 16 years. UNINHABITABLE IN 16 YEARS! Some scientists say that it could be as long as 50 years . . . The scientists do not argue about if it is going to happen, just when. I don't know about you, but I was planning on a better kind of ending than extinction. . . We, humankind, are destroying this beautiful world. The earth has lost 3/4 of its trees. We will turn 62% of the earth's land surfaces to desert by the year 2000. The average temperature will rise 9 degrees in 40 years. There is hardly any water that is not polluted. The air is downright dangerous at times. The farmland is being depleted by the chemicals that we "need". The sun is our growing enemy. Our grain reserves are way down. Many people are starving to their deaths right now.

We cannot wait for the government to do it . . . the government has not, does not, and cannot do much of anything. . . Good thoughts do not make it any more. We are fighting for our lives.

Jan Brauns Wick
Rt. 5, Box 40
Riverside, Washington, USA

If you are a politician running for office, the fact that you are a politician should disqualify you for the job.

David Coale
Palo Alto, California, USA

We don't need noble-sounding bodies of bureaucratic labyrinths. We do need institutions with teeth . . .

Dr. Mostafa K. Tolba, Exec. Dir.
U.N. Environment Programme
Budapest, Hungary

Let's hope all the various events worldwide will carry on, gathering impetus until Governments from all countries ignore us at their peril.

Karen Campbell
302 Cook Drive
Whitianga, New Zealand

The Government of Kiribati fully realizes the importance of keeping the environment in its natural state, however, like many other places, we have only given it lip service and tend to ignore it because of the economic and political implications.

> Ministry of Natural Res. Development
> P.O. Box 64
> Bairiki, Tarawa
> Republic of Kiribati

For my part, I strongly feel that it will be neither politicians (as currently self-imaged) nor environmental professionals who will begin to turn the tide against environmental degradation: it will be masses of persons most of whom have yet to understand concretely the gravity of the problems . . .

> Owen Grumbling
> Ell Pond
> Wells, Maine, USA

One last comment: I was thinking recently that perhaps if a few citizens petitioned city hall somewhere to request that a parking lot or abandoned building be converted to a swamp or wildflower sanctuary then that sort of paradigm shock would help to center America where its priorities should be.

> John Tal
> Rochester Hills, Michigan, USA

The Costa Rican Government has wisely brought . . . the issue of sustainable development . . . back into the moral sphere rather than the political, which is where it is intended to be.

> University For Peace
> P.O. Box 199-1250
> Escazu, Costa Rica, C. A.

"When the people lead, the leaders will follow."

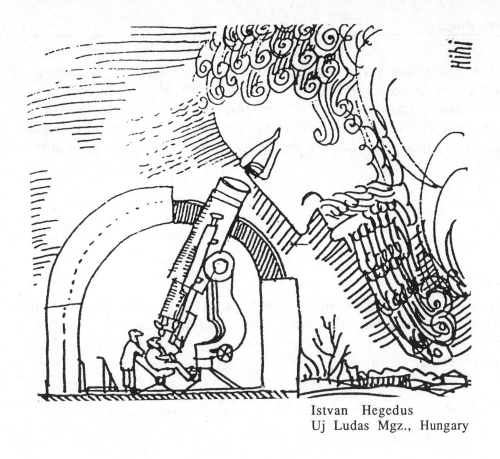

Istvan Hegedus
Uj Ludas Mgz., Hungary

8.   Stewardship

Like mighty peaks around a valley, the religions of the world encircle and spiritually protect us. At the head of the valley, where all the peaks come together, there is a high alpine meadow. Not as lofty as the peaks nor as bounteous as the valley, this pass, which leads from the valley and through the mountains, still has vegetation and still provides some protection, but is a little closer to the Infinite. Along such a favorable pathway we might all advance together, to reach a new and better land beyond.

In the past few years, Christian churches around the globe have begun to realize that part of God's call is this day to save the earth. Many ecological thinkers have accused the biblical tradition for the earth's problems because of the emphasis on the dominion of humans and its charge to "subdue the earth." In Genesis 2:15 we are asked to "tend the garden."

Reverend Micki Pulley
708 E. Loren
Springfield, Missouri, USA

We are designing our service around the theme of God as the owner of earth's wondrous garden and humankind as the caretakers of his property.

We believe that responsible care of the earth is not just a practical or material concern but is itself an ethical issue, and that religious faith which does not encompass one's dealings with his or her environment is escapist and inadequate.

Rev. Raymond E. Lambert
First Christian Church
Torrance, California, USA

There is something fundamentally wrong with Man, particularly with the present-day Western Civilization. The root cause and also the cure was spelled out by Buddha 2500 years ago: It is . . . Greed. And the cure is the eightfold path . . . essentially it is simplicity in life . . .

Ashok Shimpi
Topeka, Kansas, USA

Modern society will find no solution to the ecological problem unless it takes a serious look at its lifestyle. In many parts of the world, society is given to instant gratification and consumerism while remaining indifferent to the damage which these cause.

Pope John Paul II
Speech, January 1, 1990

. . . at our last Annual Meeting, we voted to become a 'Whole Earth Church", which means that we will take very seriously and intentionally a whole variety of suggestions the goal of which are more simple lifestyles, advocacy for a clean environment, and finding ways in the life of our congregation to renew and preserve creation.

Betty Edson, Pastor
Sharon Congregational Church
Sharon, Vermont, USA

We must salute the divinity of Earth. Take only for sustenance and only for fulfilling human needs and not (for) greed. Now is (the) time for a new model of thinking . . .

Spiritual and ecological values in our life can shape the road towards harmony, peace, and understanding of human personality. Humanity shall have to move towards a new level of consciousness (in order) to survive in universal harmony . . .

The capability of choosing our destiny thus lies within us.

The future will belong to those who are contemplative . . .

Dr. G. M. Oza
International Society of Naturalists
Oza Building, Salatwada
Baroda, - 390 001, India

*I would like to bring to your attention a 3000 year old Jewish tradition which could contribute to your endeavor. On the seventh day of the week, the Shabbat (from Friday sunset until Saturday sunset), **work** is prohibited. The major forbidden **work** is the creation of **fire**. So, for one day a week, orthodox Jews cannot drive their cars or use electrical appliances of any kind (since a spark is considered **fire**.)*

In addition to simply saving energy, this tradition makes us aware of our dependence on modern appliances and frees us for one day from machines. The result is quite nice: family and friends get closer to each other, and everyone takes a break from the rat race.

Dr. Avraham Levy
Palo Alto, California, USA

Environmental protection and the Earth Day celebrations of the 90's decade is an idea whose time has come and no forces of technological barbarism or hedonistic materialism is now going to stop this avalanche from reaching its logical conclusion in inculcating again the spirit of the reverence of Earth and all life. This completes the circle started off by the Nature Worship of our forefathers.

Sarosh Framroze
Order of the Servants of the Earth
Framroze Court - Flat No. 1
205, Marine Drive
Bombay 400 020, India

Please send me information about Earth Day celebrations in my area. I'm a pagan who wants to be involved.
Thanks! Bright Blessings!

K.W.
Greenville, Michigan, USA

We are contemplating having an Earth Day activity at our church. We don't think that our minister would be reluctant to use the Gaia concept in his Earth Day sermon, so we'd like to get stuff on that too if you've got it.

USA

We want to encourage Buddhists to develop ways of living that are ecologically sensitive and sustainable and to draw on the rich heritage of teachings that support an interdependent understanding of the world. We feel certain that the wisdom and compassion of the Buddhist teachings offers appropriate context for reviewing the nature of our relationships with living beings and the environment.
May we use the wonderful opportunity of EARTH DAY 1990 to deeply observe and appreciate our connection with all life and to participate in activities that will sustain our life for many generations.
Yours in the Dharma.

Buddhist Peace Fellowship
P.O. Box 4650
Berkeley, California, USA

The Parish of St. Stephen's, Anoka, Minnesota, joins in solidarity with those throughout the world who will celebrate this global demonstration of being concerned about the protection of the Earth.
We believe in our faith as Roman Catholics that God is the Creator of earth and everything we have comes from him. Therefore, our faith continues to challenge our Roman Catholic brothers and sisters to reach out with ethical and religious values to affect and sustain our Earth.

Reverend James A. Vedro, OSC
516 School Street
Anoka, Minnesota, USA

Through Earth Day 1990, I would hope that all peoples of the Earth, Christian or not, would give heed to the moaning and groaning of the globe as it comes under severe environmental pressure in our high-tech, throw-away society.

There is no question but what we are beginning to sensitize more and more people about the tremendous task that is ours.

C. M. Higgins, Jr.
2055 "E." Street
Lincoln, Nebraska, USA

GIBRALTAR: The high point of Earth Day celebrations will be an inter-denominational ceremony in the city's main square . . . conducted by leaders of the Christian, Jewish, Muslim, and Hindu communities.

Vanya Walker-Leigh
P.O. Box 486
Gibraltar

It is most appropriate that April 22nd is also the annual commemoration of the Holocaust for the Jewish communities. It is apparent to many of us that we are now witnessing a parallel environmental holocaust of many other life-forms on this planet and again man is the perpetrator either through ignorance or intent.

We are now in the process of setting up a special Synagogue committee to address this issue and will want to share our concerns and approach with the broader religious community both Jewish and non-Jewish.

Alan Elfanbaum
12315 Promenade
St. Louis, Missouri, USA

We join people around the world who want to be a part of giving the gift of a safer environment to future generations.

Reverend Thomas Pederson
1123 S. Kimberly Avenue
Iron Mountain, Michigan, USA

22 APRIL 1990 – EARTH DAY

ECOLOGICAL MOVEMENT
OF ST. FRANCIS OF ASISI – CRACOW

Poland

. . . the importance of the Earth to our life and well being . . . has most recently exploded into our consciousness and is evoking creative responses all over Mother Earth. One of the consequences of this has been a new understanding of the interconnectedness with one another and with the whole of creation. I would like to recognize and support the celebration of Earth Day 1990 as a slice of time when citizens of this globe will be in solidarity with one another . . . (We) anticipated the day with a Spring Equinox "Planting for a New Earth."

"Earthings" directed by
Sister Jane Pellowski &
Sister Estelle Demers
Philadelphia, Pennsylvania, USA

. . . the members of St. Anthony's Fraternity . . . wish to affiliate themselves & our Fraternity with Earth Day 1990.

We do so as Catholics dedicated to the gospel message of good stewardship of all creation, and as Secular Franciscans whose Rule of Life calls us to "respect all creatures, animate and inanimate, which 'bear the imprint of the Most High,'" and "to move from the temptation of exploiting creation to the Franciscan concept of universal kinship."

May each of us deepen our commitment to protect our fellowman and the planet on which we live.

Theresa A. Leone, SFO, Fraternity Minster
Philadelphia, Pennsylvania USA

God has allowed us to grow in knowledge so that we can even hurl ourselves into space and circulate among the planets. One thing we have seen from those journeys is that we are unique in His creation . . . Shouldn't we praise the Lord for this gift of creation by maintaining it?

Nancy Romans Tinnell
Middletown United Methodist Church
Middletown, Kentucky, USA

My soul can find no staircase to Heaven unless it be through Earth's loveliness.

Michelangelo

. . . the Society of Jesus wishes to join their voices with those of many others who are trying to raise consciousness about global and environmental degradation. We consider it one of the most important social, ethical, and justice issues facing men and women of our generation. Our failure to address this issue will be a serious injustice to our children and to all future generations.

USA

Buddhist Peace Fellowship
P.O. Box 4650
Berkeley, California, USA

(Earth Day has) a wonderful vision, upon which governments of the Earth and her people must wake up and take action. You have the fullest support of my organization and myself.

God bless our planet Earth; god bless your pure mind and vision.

Captain Geofrey Kiendi
Development University Church
Africa Projects Association
P.O. Box 62333, Nairobi, Kenya

Please let us know what we can do here in York, PA. Just us kids on our street. God has given us a Good Earth; we have just let things get out of hand. I pray it's not too late for our kids. . . God made the Sun, Earth, Moon, and Stars; we are to enjoy not destroy.

All God's children are one.

D.L.T.
USA

. . . I feel if I really am ever going to accomplish anything in this world, I must start standing up for my beliefs and do something about them! Instead of just thinking or talking or hoping they'll happen. I may not be powerful or have much money, but I can do what I think is right. I am only 16 years old but I believe somehow, even in the smallest ways, I can make a difference, in my life and others.

I haven't done much for my world concerning the pollutions and homeless and such, but now I'm at the point where I want to do as much as I can for everyone and everything because I'm tired of sitting around and waiting. I can do whatever I try to do and this world is my world too, so I should do whatever I can to make it better. I can't really explain the feelings that are overwhelming me but I feel I have to say and do something or I am going to explode! And most of all let myself down.

There's one thing that hasn't been mentioned . . . That is, maybe one big thing that can help us all accomplish our goals in anything including making people aware of the earth's problems and giving them inspiration to change, and that is God. I feel prayer and closeness to him has played a big part in my life and he's probably the reason I have become so concerned and enthusiastic about helping others out. If only one person reads this, then I have begun to make a difference.

I hope I can make a difference, no matter what I do. I hope we all can!!!

Rebekah Montgomery
P.O. Box 72
East Corondelet, Illinois, USA

I am very concerned about the fact that we are destroying our gift from God, Earth. I am starting to realize that if I don't take action now, we won't have anything left.

Mellissa Johnson
500 Airport Road
Jonesville, Louisiana, USA

. . . the scheduled Earth Day falls during the holiest month of Ramadan, a month of praying and thanks to Almighty for His gifts and mercy. Especially . . . the 22nd falls on the 27th of Ramadan (the most important religious day in the Kingdom and the Islamic world) called "Lailathul Qadr" wherein all Muslims throughout the world spend the whole night in prayers and reciting the Holy Book. All the people are in a festive mood, eagerly awaiting Eid day (the 26th or 27th of April). . . with this mood in the hearts of Muslims in the Kingdom, it is very difficult to fully participate in all the programs envisaged by the Earth Day campaign . . .

King Abdulaziz City for Science and
Technology
Kingdom of Saudi Arabia

I am concerned with the environment and preserving its natural beauty. It is what's most important to me in life. Nature is what I live for when everything else in life falls apart. We have God and nature to turn to for joy and memories.

Nancy J. McLaughlin
649 E. 194th Street
Glenwood, Illinois, USA

To my fellow inhabitants of this planet, I say let us each take up the good fight to preserve and protect this precious gift, our Earth.

Reverend Jeff Knighton
701 Main Street
Scott City, Kansas, USA

Too little to see
Over tops of trees
Too little to be heard
Over people so big

Too little to see
No one saw as I cried
But I am not too little
to see me standing
By the Lord's side.

Glory Andrea Rhinehart
Rd. #2, Box 745
Georgia, Vermont, USA

Chaplain Charles Shirley
The Interfaith Airport Chaplaincy
Atlanta International Airport
Atlanta, Georgia, USA

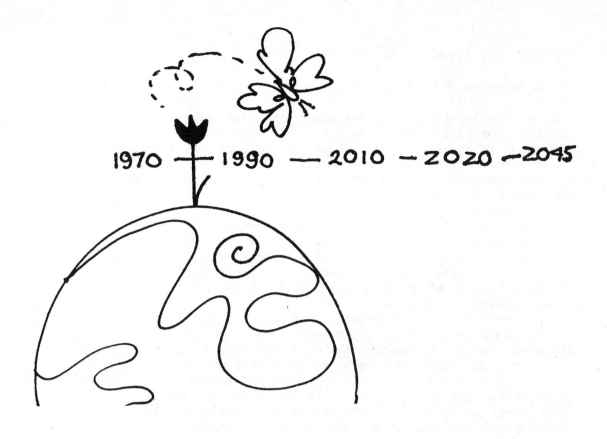

1970 — 1990 — 2010 — 2020 — 2045

Jane Engelman
Los Angeles, California, USA

9. Ceremonies and Celebrations

All the announcement said was "Earth Day is April 22." That 200 million people responded says not so much about the five words as it says about the needs of people everywhere to let out frustrations and share hopes. Despite some doubts about the effectiveness of a celebration, despite some anxieties about the cost, despite some religious and political obstacles, and even despite war, death, and revolution, people did celebrate the Tag der Erde, the Dia de la Tierra. How they chose to demonstrate, whether practically or ritualistically, was not dictated by the Earth Day Headquarters, but came from the individuals in communities, each with its own particular needs and worries. Between the loner who planted trees in his back yard and the million and a half fans who filled the streets and parks of New York city were hundreds of thousands of celebrants with private stories of meaningful events.

An Earth Day Appeal

>From Minamata to the People of the World

On this day, Earth Day, we gather here in Minamata City
and call upon all our friends throughout the world to take a
stand with us under the slogan "Eliminate pollution and protect the
global environment!"   This appeal comes to you from the site of
the first appearance of Minamata disease, an affliction said to be
the genesis of pollution.
Our earth is suffering.   Unrestricted industrial
activities have resulted in the depletion of the ozone layer by CFCs and
global warming due to an increase in carbon dioxide, not to
mention the growing danger presented by tens of thousands of toxic and
hazardous substances, the logging of the rainforests, and
desertification, all of which indisputably leave the future
of our descendants in doubt.
Another of these phenomena is the worldwide spread of
environmental contamination by mercury, the cause of
Minamata disease, thus manifesting signs that "the Minamata tragedy"
is occurring in many other countries throughout the world.
Our earth is the foundation of survival for not only all
human beings and their descendants on the planet, but for all
living things, and it is the shared plea of all humanity that we
eliminate pollution and protect the global environment.
Minamata disease was officially discovered 34 years ago on
May 1.   Today even Japan's courts have recognized that
Minamata disease occurred as a result of Japan's corporate and
government industrial policies, which grant precedence to the economy
and production.
However, while in Japan there are over 2,000 Minamata
disease patients, the government claims they "do not have
Minamata disease," and refuses to offer them redress.
Everyone in Japan believes that since the Japanese
government cannot even solve the Minamata disease problem -- the
genesis of pollution, Japan is not qualified to speak on global
pollution and environmental problems as "a nation with advanced pollution
control technology."
In our way of thinking, the most important thing is not
corporate activities and industrial policies that favor
economics, but the preservation of the global environment, not to
mention human activities that grant precedence to the lives and
health of present and future human beings.
We believe that the wish for "No More Minamata" goes hand
in hand with the desire to pass this abundant earth on to our
descendants, and once again we call upon people all over
the world to "Eliminate pollution and protect the global
environment!"

Japan

I remember April 22, 1970 vividly: Along with hundreds of other high school students, I marched the streets of Omaha, Nebraska with a gas mask on to make a statement about clean air. I want to make this 20th anniversary even more memorable!

M. L. King
Spokane, Washington, USA

It is with great excitement that I approach Earth Day 1990! Twenty years ago I celebrated the first Earth Day as a fourth grader in Indianola, Iowa. This year I am teaching fourth graders in Springtown, Texas. I still remember, twenty years later, our childhood excitement at picking up trash and litter on our large school yard under the direction of Mrs. Conley, our teacher. I wish to instill a genuine concern for our environment in my fourth grade class.

Lisa Goben
Weatherford, Texas, USA

Seems I remember Earth Day (1970) at San Jose State . . . Didn't we bury a small car next to the old student cafeteria . . . ?

Andrea Whitehurst
Magnolia Forest
Pungo, Virginia, USA

(In 1970) I was involved in a sit-in at my high school which resulted in threats and suspensions and my parents coming in for consultation. I think schools are better educated now.

Michael Benedetto
Hillsbro Rd. R 17
Camden, New York, USA

WHEN I WAS IN COLLEGE IN KY., I WAS A MEMBER OF THE ENVIRONMENTAL STUDIES CLUB, AND WE OBSERVED EARTH DAY BY DOING A VARIETY OF WONDERFUL, FULFILLING ACTIVITIES. WE USUALLY BEGAN THE NIGHT BEFORE, CAMPING OUT ATOP LOCKAGEE ROCK, A SORT OF "LOOKOUT POINT," LOCATED IN MOREHEAD, KY, AND A PART OF THE DANIEL BOONE NATIONAL FORREST, I BELIEVE. EARTH DAY STARTED WITH A SUNRISE BREAKFAST ATOP THE MOUNTAIN, WITH GUITAR SOLOS, HOMEMADE GOODIES TO EAT, AND A SUNRISE WORSHIP SERVICE. WE GAVE THANKS FOR THE SPLENDOR AND BEAUTY EVIDENT FOR MILES IN EVERY DIRECTION. THE REMAINDER OF THE DAY WAS DEVOTED TO SUCH PROJECTS AS LOCAL CLEAN-UPS, TREE-PLANTING, ETC., AND WE MANNED AN INFORMATION BOOTH NEAR THE STUDENT CENTER FOR ANY WHO MIGHT WANT TO KNOW MORE. LATER WE HAD A SCRUMPTIOUS PICNIC, AND WHEN DARKNESS CAME, WE HAD A CANDLELIGHT MARCH ACROSS THE CAMPUS. THE MARCH ENDED IN FRONT OF OUR MAJESTIC LIBRARY, WHERE A LOCAL BAND PLAYED FOLK MUSIC WHILE WE LOUNGED ON THE GROUND BENEATH THE TREES. I STILL RECALL THOSE DAYS WITH PLEASURE, AND WITH SADNESS, TOO, BECAUSE HERE IN ORLANDO, PEOPLE JUST DON'T SEEM TO CARE. I HAVE BEEN HERE ALMOST SIX YEARS, AND HAVE NEVER SEEN ANY TYPE OF CELEBRATION TO SHOW THAT EARTH DAY EVEN EXISTS. I HOPE THAT I AM JUST SO MUCH OUT OF SYNC WITH THE EVERYDAY EVENTS HERE THAT I SIMPLY AM NOT AWARE OF THE PROJECTS THAT HAVE BEEN PLANNED, WHICH IS WHY I IMMEDIATELY WANTED TO WRITE YOU WHEN I SAW YOUR ADDRESS IN THE WORKING MOTHER MAGAZINE.

ALSO, I WOULD APPRECIATE KNOWING HOW I COULD PURCHASE A COUPLE OF THE GREEN EARTH DAY T-SHIRTS THAT WERE PICTURED IN THE SAME MAGAZINE. PERHAPS I COULD EVEN INTEREST SOME OF MY CO-WORKERS IN THEM AS WELL!

I DO NOT HAVE VERY MUCH MONEY TO INVEST IN ENVIRONMENTAL PROJECTS, HAVING JUST HAD AN ADDITION TO OUR FAMILY, BUT I DO GIVE AS MUCH AS I POSSIBLY CAN. IF I COULD JUST GET MORE INVOLVED THEN I WOULD AT LEAST FEEL AS IF I WERE DOING SOMETHING WORHTWHILE. IF YOU ARE AWARE OF ANY ENVIRONMENTAL GROUPS IN MY AREA WHO COULD BENEFIT FROM A FEW HOURS OF MY TIME TO DO PAPERWORK, TYPING, STUFFING MAIL, ETC., PLEASE SEND THIS AS WELL. I SHALL ANXIOUSLY AWAIT YOUR REPLY.

Sincerely,
Elizabeth L. Palowitch

Elizabeth L. Palowitch
7200 Ferrara Avenue
Orlando, Florida, USA

I am ten years old and in the fourth grade . . . I am in the Student Council and we are doing something special for Earth Day. We are going to find out what each member of the faculty is going to give up to help save the earth . . .

Jonathan Mark Lucke
Springridge   Elementary
Richardson, Texas, USA

Greetings and peace from Ireland! Earth Day . . . is something I don't think is celebrated here, not in Cork anyway . . . Even if it's only myself standing on a street corner holding a flag, I want to celebrate my planet and declare my love for this beautiful world we live in.

David McGilton
Bishoptown, Cork, Ireland

Greetings from Azerbaijan. Yes, friends, our Earth is in danger. Mankind is threatened by a catastrophe. The greater the effort of us, teachers and adults, to raise children with desire to plant a tree or an orchard, the cleaner will be the air of our planet.

I work in a school of 1300 children . . . how about getting together on Earth Day, to see our children meet your children and plant trees together?

Ashirov Gulspaj Abdulovna
School 3, KUD
Village Hyrdalan, Apsheronsky
Azerbaijan 373250, USSR

Colton Elementary School will have an Earth Day celebration on April 20. The band will play and all the classes K-6 will observe a tree being planted on our playground. Some students will share poems they have written or short stories. Mrs. Stanchfield's 5th grade class will present a play about trees. During our celebration, or rather the conclusion of the celebration, will be the passing down of a ball that represents the earth from adult staff down to the 6th grade and 5th grade and on down to the Kindergarten--passing the earth down to the children.

USA

Already we have planned a tree planting to honor members of our class who have died in the past 2 years.

105th Street Advocates
United Cerebral Palsy/ Spastic Children's
Foundation
Los Angeles, California, USA

The Ceremony will begin with a two-minute silence . . . for each member to ponder on how he or she could contribute in the coming years to the three principles of Earth Day which are PEACE, DEVELOPMENT, AND THE ENVIRONMENT. This will be followed by prayers and the Earth Day pledge . . . (and) the ringing of our 18-year-old Earth Day peace bell which we acquired for our first Earth Day Observance in 1972. Earth Day peace birds will be released to be followed by cheers and "Happy Earth Day" handshakes, one with all members and friends present.

Dr. Tommy Kwik
Planetary Citizen's Council
Robinson Road, PO Box 2753
Singapor, 9047

When is Earth Day? I looked for it on my calendar and couldn't find it. Does it get recognized on any calendars? I should think it's more important than a lot of holidays recognized on my calendar.

Kim Bresler
Mountain Grove
Missouri, USA

On Sunday, April 22, San Diegans can run for the planet in the first annual Rainforest Run. The event, co-hosted by the San Diego Zoo (critters included) and local radio station Y95, will officially kick-off the day-long fest at Balboa Park. Every $50 raised in the run will purchase, for conservation, one acre of rainforest in the Central American country of Belize.

Rainforest Run
3860 Chippewa Court
San Diego, California, USA

*Hello! My name is Katie Gill, I am 16 years old. I am
very involved in saving OUR EARTH! I am so excited about
Earth Day 1990! Here is my schedule for Earth Day:*

am 4:00-5:30 - Meditation and Breakfast

am 5:30-6:00 - Get dressed

am 6:30-7:00 - Watch sunrise. Pray

*am 7:00-9:00 - Go around neighborhood to find and
collect trash*

*am 9:00-2:00 - At local Earth Day activity - Cleaning up
a park & planting trees.*

pm 2:00-2:30 - Drop off food at local Humane Society

*pm 2:30-3:00 Go around neighborhood to collect
recyclable goods*

*pm 3:00-5:30 - Go stand in line at recycling center and
help separate goods and weigh*

pm 5:30-6:00 Eat quick

pm 6:00-9:00 Go pick up trash around freeway

*pm 9:00-11:00 Friends and I are playing "Seek a Trash."
I have a field behind my house, and I got a group
of 15 friends together and in the dark with
flashlights, light clothing, and trash bags we will
see who can pick up most trash. (We have
permission from field owner.)*

11:30 - Think over what I did today!

12:00 - I'm pooped. Time for bed.

*This is my schedule. I hope most people will take this
day seriously!*

Katie Scarlet Gill
Newark, Ohio, USA

In . . . Vac the organizers will roll a huge globe through town. In the capital--Budapest--dozens of events will take place. Several thousands of cyclists are expected at the bike demonstration against the air pollution. Members of the Voks Humana movement protest against the devastation of the tropical rainforests by passing a coffin full of sawdust to the Brazilian ambassador.

Hungary

On another day, we hope to put gravestones on the school lawn every hour, signifying the deaths of endangered species.

Robert W. Gee
3204 Hobcaw Lane
Lexington, KY   40502

In upper Silesia . . . people have proposed to form a chain of life around the most polluted area which is known as the Death Triangle of Europe. We do not want to organize this event only and then stop. But we do want to start a new life with the 1990-2000 decade of sustainable growth. This for sure should be done if we all want to survive.

Poland

The resident Council representing our 200 patients wishes to demonstrate concern for future generations by celebrating "Earth Day" . . . Our members are primarily in their late eighties and early nineties, so there is no doubt that the concern is for generations yet to come. Though realistically many of our members do not expect to witness the year two thousand, there is an intense desire to envision a benign future . . .

Rose Rosett, C.T.R.S.
Bronx, New York, USA

At the American research station at the geographic South Pole, on the antarctic ice sheet and in darkness until September, the 20 winterers cleaned up and had a day of slides at the remote spot. The slides included pictures they brought down with them--flowers, landscapes, sunrises, clouds . . . They're in complete isolation from February 'til November.

At McMurdo . . . many braved a wind chill of minus 65 to clean up outdoors: they took 15 trucks of trash to the station's waste sorting area.

USA

We are also excited at the tremendous possibilities open to all of us to reflect, create, rejoice, be hopeful . . . to act together towards a Common Cause. Indeed, we are wondering where we get the courage and determination to embark on such an ambitions project considering "our pockets are empty, only our hearts are full."

Elin B. Mondejar
SEARICE
P.O.Box EA - 31 Ermita
Manila, Philippines

Here, in our economically devastated community, traditionally dependent upon coal mining, environmental issues are not in the forefront. However, I would like to see Earth Day receive some recognition even if it is only in the form of an informative letter to our local paper.

Mary Ann Andera
1420 S. Fourth St.
Raton, New Mexico, USA

Dear Earth Day Headquarters,

The celebration of the 20th anniversary of Earth Day was a fabulous event and those of us who worked on Earth Day activities in our communities are still excited about carrying on the environmental message.

We are very disappointed however with the national Earth Day headquarters because we had no support in the manner of any publicity or financial backing for our local events even though many people from our community sent donations to the national Earth Day Headquarters. It appears that our contribution dollars were spent in large cities with no regards for small communities.

In a town of 42,000 people, one hundred thirty-three grassroots volunteers raised $52,000 needed to stage more than 150 events, produce an environmental video, and an Earth Day Concert and Fair. We did not take one penny from large corporations who are primary polluters such as Pacific Gas and Electric or any oil company. All our donations were small. The owners of the concert and fair sight were amazed that not one piece of trash could be found the following day. The garbage company claimed that so little garbage was put into the dumpsters they are still wondering what we did with the trash--we recycled and composted.

Those same hundred and thirty-three volunteers met last night and their numbers has attracted more to join in the effort to keep the spirit and message of Earth Day alive in San Luis Obispo. We are asking that you re-evaluate many of the things that happened with the hope that we can look to you for support and guidance in the future.

Respectfully,

Ilona Ing

Ilona Ing

Ilona Ing
S.L.O. Earth Day Coalition
San Luis Obispo, California, USA

Earth Day - Burma
c/o P. O. Box 89
Mae Sot   Post. No. 63110
Tak Province   Date 1.3.90
Thailand.

Dear Friends,

   I'm sorry for the slowness of our response, it is partly due to the disruption of our planned activities with the ABSDF 'Jungle University' by the overrunning of our camps by the Burmese army. We are now planning to undertake Earth Day activities in refugee camps along the border of Burma and Thailand. We hope we will be able to place Burma on the environmental map - it is certainly a land in crisis and needs as much attention as possible. We also hope that we can be listed among those who care for our environment as those are who are included in your international update. We are truly sorry to not be carrying out our environmental actions in Burma instead of in a refugee camp in Thailand.

   Anyway, what we plan to do, if we are given permission by the Thai authorities, is to hold a "Funeral for the Forests - A Day of Mourning and Hope." To show our hope for the future, our determination not to succumb to despair, and to remind ourselves of what has gone before, we will plant as many trees as possible on this day. We will establish plant nurseries, if the Thai officials will allow it, to raise plants to grow in Thailand

8mm

We will grow trees to replace those we have cut down to make shelters here and to replace those we have cut, or will cut, for firewood or other uses. We would like to grow fruit trees in case we cannot return to Burma soon. We do not wish to be accused of forest destruction in Thailand. We would like to show a positive attitude by planting trees both for ourselves, for the local peoples' benefit, and for the Earth. The Karen people have seen their forests being torn down around them in the last year as a result of the Burmese military government's policy. This policy is to sell the forests (and fishing and mining rights) to the Thai government in return for money, international recognition (which it doesn't deserve), a convenient set of access roads for the army to use into the once inaccessible, defensible forests, and other services and benefits. Thus have war, economics, politics, and environmental destruction worked against the Karen peoples and the other ethnic minorities of Burma. Without the forest, the Karen people truly lack shelter.

On Earth Day, if the Thai authorities allow it, and if we can raise the resources to carry it out, we would like to plant 200,000 trees. We need to quickly find some capital for a water pump, nursery equipment, and planting tools. It may be understood that our resources are mostly those of skills, will, and muscle, rather than money. However, we will do our best.

We would like to establish plant nurseries in all the camps along the border eventually, but initially we will confine our efforts to two. In one camp . . . we will undertake to grow, both for Earth Day and for a future supply, seedlings of fruit trees, fast growing nitrogen-fixing trees for food, fuelwood, and construction materials, and a range of others like teak, rosewood, and some of the many dipterocarps endemic to the region.

Another aspect of our Earth Day effort, other than the ceremonies for those killed in defending the forest and for the forests themselves, is our education program. We would like to reestablish the 'Jungle University' program in the refugee camps (if possible) to teach the "Environmental Awareness Training" course that was suspended because of the attacks. However, permission has not been granted for this. Instead, those involved in the plant nursery will receive training in nursery techniques, reasons for fire prevention, correct rubbish disposal, composting, and the use of plants for shade, nitrogen fixing, fodder, etc.

We will encourage the wearing of both black and green armbands on Earth Day to symbolize both mourning and hope. Burma has totally inadequate environmental law, rapidly disappearing rainforest, an army of international companies itching to devour her "rich natural resources", some of the most heavily silted rivers in the world, a rich and beautiful variety of wildlife that is virtually unprotected, Thai tin dredgers destroying the coastline, a growing dry zone in the central plains, and a host of others. We feel that the world knows virtually nothing of the realities of Burma. We think it would be good if this situation was to change.

Mae Sot
Tak Province, Thailand

On Earth Day in Long Beach we had a crowd of over 20,000 on our beach for the program . . . It was a total success, and done without the aid of any politicians or money exchangers. A free event, with people that willingly donated their time and energy, and a feeling of love and cooperation that permeated the crowd that day . . .

I am enclosing copies of the local news stories on it for you to . . . show the rest of the world what can be achieved on the local level, with a handful of dedicated people, regular, every day citizens.

I truly feel that this movement will continue to snowball, and we can and will make a difference!

Maria Heller
540 W. Penn Street
Long Beach, New York, USA

. . . remember: we'll all be with you in Ellis, Kansas, on April 22. We'll be wearing our T-shirts and planting trees!

Marlene Dinkel
701 St. Mary's
Ellis, Kansas, USA

On the 22nd it was cloudy in Hungary, but it could not kill the Earth Day. The whole day was beyond our expectations. 100,000 people marching in the streets dressed in green clothes, or riding the bicycles, a full program on Hungarian television, a 20 hour program on the radio. We can say: Earth Day resounded through the country. Hungarian people were conscious of the importance of the day.

Judit Vasarhelyi & Gyorgy Pal Gado
H-1525 P.O. Box 32
Budapest, Hungary

. . . in Five Major Thoroughfares in Metro Manila, 780 Smoke Belchers (motor vehicles) were apprehended and had their registration plates confiscated.

Amando C. Dayrit
Anti-smoke Belching Project
Philippines

We made a paper chain on recycled grocery bags. On each chain we listed something we would personally do to keep the earth green and clean.

Deborah A. Langford
Diamond Valley School
35 Hawkside Drive
Markleeville, California, USA

In honor of Earth Day '90, my husband and I purchased three shade trees to plant in our yard--one to dedicate to each of our three sons. (We) will plant them Sun. April 22 and explain as we do that each tree will put us the tiniest bit closer to clean air, less reliance on air conditioning . . . and a healthier Earth for the kids that these trees represent.

Hopefully, they'll outlive all of us and serve as a symbol of our family's commitment to our world!

Laura Kay Goraj
Dearborn Heights.
Michigan, USA

. . . then we planted a tree for each grade level. The children "blessed" the trees and received "blessings" from the trees. This was the one thing many of them talked about with their parents.

Gracia Valliant
Bloomington, Indiana, USA

. . . about the recent Earth Day Celebration. It was a beautiful thing to see, all the energy and concern from nation to nation. I pray it lasts.

Joan M. Padilla
Sterling, Illinois, USA

African Centre for Science and Development Information , P.O. Box 3616, Yaba, Lagos. Nigeria.

Courier delivery: 5, Efunboye Street, Off Shyllon Street, Palmgrove, Lagos, Nigeria. Telephone (01) 824353

On behalf of the local organising committee of **Earth Day 1990**, in Nigeria, I here report that we in Nigeria, marked **Earth Day** the first time ever, despite the fact that Nigeria's bloodiest coup attempt was made here on the morning of Sunday April 22.

It was this sheer serenpidity that saw Nigeria joining the world in marking Earth Day. For barely six hours after government officials and notable environmentalists in the country declared open our activities which included the country's first-ever photographic exhibition on the _State of the Environment_, at the Nigerian Institute of International Affairs in Lagos, a mutinous clique of soldiers stormed the Dodan Barracks seat of the Nigerian military government. The barracks is barely two kilometres away from the venue of the exhibition.

We had gone ahead with our activities for **Earth Day '90** despite the dangerous situation in the country because of our firm belief that even though a coup, like a government, may have substantial impact on life and living in our country, no such changes can have anything near as permanent an effect as the deterioration, devastation and other changes in the Environment today, will have on life on Earth henceforth.

Without necessarily being insensitive to the dicey political situation in our country, we found supporting evidence for our position in the fact that not even the October 1917 Revolution of the Soviet Union outlasted a whole generation.

We remain yours,

O'seun Ogunseitan
Co-ordinator

An independent specialised information agency working from Africa for
the promotion of Science and sustainable development worldwide.
Executive Director: O'Seun Ogunseitan

BAHAMAS NATIONAL TRUST

EARTH WEEK April 22-28, 1990

PO Box N-4105, Nassau, Bahamas Ph. 393-1317

ACT NOW!

What a week we had! I can only say that the successes of Earth Week were more than we ever hoped for or imagined.

It began on April 21 with our island-wide, community-wide clean-up campaign. On that day we collected 200 tons of litter from across New Providence. What we thought might be a logistical mightmare turned out to be a heavy machinery ballet. Everything ran so smoothly; the community involvement was unprecedented; the amount of litter collected was extraordinary; and, the impression we made on the Government will, I am sure, be lasting. The Department of Environmental Health has gone so far as to solicit our assistance in up-coming clean-up programs of their own.

Our Earth Week, which ran from April 22 - 28, was filled with similar successes. The opening ceremony turned out to be a forum from which Government announced new environmental policies. The Adelaide Creek Wetlands Restoration Project stimulated a forgotten, grassroots community - whose roots lie in the emancipation of slaves in the early 1800's - and brought the most diverse members of our community together, working side by side to restore the environment.

Community involvement contributed much to the success of Earth Week. Rotarians became the workforce with which our tree planting project was launched. At the official tree planting ceremony with H.R.H. Prince Edward, the Prime Minister asked the National Trust to organised Earth Week every year. Yesterday, at a major Tourism Conference, he even suggested that what the Bahamas needed most was an earth year!

I wish there was some way to impress upon you the scope of our successes. The Bahamas National Trust, founded thirty years ago, has never really enjoyed Government's full support... for the first time we were able to rise above that and achieve many things. In our thirty-year history the Prime Minister never attended a single Trust function. During Earth Week he attended three.

Best Wishes,

Susan Larson

MT. RAINIER • EARTH DAY 1990

"*Think Globally* • *Act Locally*"

4/20

Dear Earth Day 1990 —

Please put us down on the
master list as having honored
Earth Day.

WE DID IT! ALL OVER!
Now for the more sobering,
less heady long haul.

Thanks for your leadership.

Steve McKindley-Ward
Chair, Mt. Rainier Earth Day Committee

Steve McKindley-Ward
4112 30th Street
Mt. Rainier, Maryland, USA

Earth Foundation, Australia

10. Poems, Pledges, and Songs

I walk outside when it's dark at night
I look up at the sky--what a sight!
The moon is so bright;
The stars shine much light;
The air feels just right;
What a beautiful night!

Raymond Tautic
Clover Street School
Windsor, Connecticut, USA

We got the fires that
ate up Yellowstone,
we got the floods that
sank Bangladesh--we got--
miles of needles
down the
East Coast beaches.
We got the
prodigal barge
of trash . . .

We got
to guard the
garden planet--
Keep it nice,
and green--
--of the fifty
million billion
worlds out there . . .
. . . It's the only garden planet
*   we've seen . . .*

We got the Swiss cheese
of the ozone.
*   We got--*
--smoke--
--we got smog . . .
We got sludge,
We got people--
--pullin power when nobody's home . . .
We got no one
pullin' power
from the wind
and the sun--!

We got people pullin' power
from all over town--
We got
people
flushin' water
when the power
breaks down.

And when the power
*   breaks down . . .*
Gonna be a
hot-house,
baby:
a hot-house, baby--
We're gonna sweat,
the whole world wide.
A hot-house, baby--
we'll never dare
to step outside.

We've got to
guard
. . . the garden planet:
keep it nice--
and green.

Of the fifty-
million billion
worlds out there . . .

Matt Levin for
Cindy Meise
123 Elm Street
Hatfield, Massachusetts, USA

The sky was meant to be blue
The air was meant to be clean
The water was meant to be beautiful
and animals should be roaming free.

But the sky is full of smog
and the air is full of pollution
The water is full of toxins
and animals have no solutions.

So, what we've got to do is change the earth
To the way it was meant to be
With skies that are blue
and air that is clean
with water that is beautiful
and animals that are roaming free.

Tim Brown & Pat Hsieh
Georgia, Vermont, USA

Now I'm writing this poem to say:
"Save the Rain Forests today."
I'm rather mad at what we've done,
We've cut trees which will soon be gone.
Now I'll repeat what I've already said,
"We save them now - or Rain Forests are dead."

USA

EARTH DAY APRIL 22 1990

We, the Bahá'í children of Lusaka will try to
Take care of our trees.
Put rubbish in proper bins.
Keep our yards tidy.
Make sure the taps are not left dripping.

P. KALAPWE

I PLEDGE TO DO MY SHARE IN SAVING THE PLANET
BY LETTING MY CONCERN FOR THE ENVIRONMENT SHAPE
HOW I CONSUME, PURCHASE and VOTE.

I am committed to doing my utmost to recycle, conserve energy, save water, use efficient transportation, remember the Earth's limitations if I choose to have a family, and try to adopt a lifestyle as if every day were Earth Day.

I am committed to buying and using those products least harmful to the environment. Moreover, I will to the maximum extent possible, do business with corporations that promote global environmental responsibility.

I am committed to voting for and supporting those candidates who demonstrate an abiding concern for the environment.

I am committed to supporting the passage of local, state and federal laws and international treaties that protect the environment.

Let Earth Day 1990 know that you have joined thousands of others in taking the Green Pledge.

Name (please print) _Joe Montana_   Signature _Joe M___

Address _4999 Central Blvd_

City _Santa Clara_   State _Ca_   Zip

KID'S PLEDGE

I promise to help save my planet Earth, by:
Not messing up parks, streets and other places. I won't litter.
I'll walk, ride my bike, or take a bus instead of riding in cars, whenever I can.
I'll save and recycle things like paper and cans. I'll ask my parents to be kind to our planet, too.

NAME _Diana Millward_   AGE _eight_

CITY _Peoria_   STATE _AZ_   ZIP _85381_

We are strong, we are bold;
We never let go, we always hold.
No more drugs, no more pain,
We don't need your crack cocaine.
No more violence, no more wars
We don't need your nuclear Star Wars.
Freedom of choice, abortion maybe;
We should have the choice to decide on the baby.
Look at our environment; we are going to die.
When we notice that our environment is destroyed, we will not have the time to even ask why.

Alison Martin
South Jordan, Utah, USA

Mother Nature, in anger, cries out our name
Reminding us always of our selfless shame
Moaning in the night about our waste
Caused by the hurry to grow; such haste
To be productive at the expense of Man
Purging the life from our weary land
Disregarding the balance of future existence
Oh, Mother Earth, I bow my tired head
When I see our world eroding; growing dead
Few seem to care that the world is unhealthy
As long as the greedy can grow more wealthy
I must ask myself at the dawning of each day
Who is responsible? Who has found the way?
What is the inheritance that I am leaving?
Will there be celebration or will there be grieving?
I have listened to your cry in the still night
I am ready to be counted; ready to fight
For though I may be only one amongst the throngs
I am compelled to strive to right the wrongs.
So now I pay heedance to your call
The hope indeed with me; as with all.

Thomas J. Taylor
651 S. W. 11th
Moore, Oklahoma, USA

EARTH
(H.M.P)

BY RANDALL JOHNSON

(ROCK)

Randall Johnson
Samnorwood School 1971
Wellington, Texas, USA

I pledge allegiance
to my faith
in the united soul of Humanity,
and to the earth on which we stand:
one family,
born of love,
indivisible,
with life in abundance for all.

Leila Lord *
P.O. Box 1702
Gainesville, Florida, USA

I pledge devotion
to the earth,
our one and only home,
and to the life this earth sustains: one body,
one spirit,
indivisible,
with freedom and fulfillment for all.

Bruce Robert Hagen
Petaluma, California, USA

- -

As a human being I am concerned with the quality of experience enjoyed by our species in this precious instant of life. I am also concerned with the quality of experience we allow the other living beings on the planet to enjoy.

I envision, as I am sure you do, a co-operative global community, based on the central commitment to honor life, to seek to understand and appreciate the nature of this gift, and to care for its support system--this beautiful blue-green Earth.

As a teacher I see that the realization of this vision depends directly upon our cultivation of the smaller "globes" sitting on the young shoulders of our charges. What we program in today is likely to show up in the mind-sets of tomorrow's leaders.

If we want a co-operative world, one in which the "inalienable rights" Americans hold dear accrue to everyone on earth . . . then we need to teach both ourselves and our young to think beyond my family, my race, and my nation, to our world--our one human community, on our one living earth.

As "one small step" in that direction, I have written a new "Pledge of Allegiance."

The Global Pledge of Allegiance

I pledge allegiance to the earth
And to the Universal Spirit
Which gives us Life;
One planet, indivisible,
With Peace and Justice for us all.

I pledge to do my best
To uphold the trust bestowed
In the gift of my Life;
To care for our planet and our atmosphere,
To respect and honor all her inhabitants,
All people, animals, plants and resources,
To create a legacy for our children
And our children's children
In a world of Harmony and Love.

I pledge allegiance to the Universal Spirit,
By whatever name it may be called.
I align my Life
With the ongoing process of Creation;
To grow myself with care,
To act from my own integrity,
To be for others
How I would want them to be for me.

Together,
May we carry this vision in our hearts,
Into our daily choices,
And through our expanding consciousness
Within and beyond our planet......

Edna Reitz, ©1989

23414 Clarendon Street
Woodland Hills, California, USA

It's Up To Me

R. D. Carlin

1. It's up to me to save this land, I'll save it good as an-y can;
2. I'll plant its fields and reap its grain, e-nough for me and ev-ery one;
3. Those lit-tered roads, guess I'm to blame; I've spread my trash from Nome to Maine;
4. Each beast and bird from No-ah's ark de-serves some space on which to park;

These shores and plains, the hills I love, my leg-a-cy from God a-bove.
Yet I must share its rich re-ward, for hun-ger's cost I can't af-ford.
But if they'll ev-er clean-er be, the clean-ing up is up to me.
For if I force them from their home, in time I may be forced to roam.

5.
I did not take the time to be
The parent my folks were for me;
My children gone - I count, alone,
The things I thought they'd need to own.

6.
To lead the ones that I hold dear,
I've got to keep my thinking clear;
For if I "smoke" away my soul,
There's not enough to pay the toll.

7.
It is not good to want it all,
Else, who'll be listening if I call?
If I have stacked it all for me,
What neighbor will my neighbor be?

8.
This earth: my home; it's Heaven's womb,
And I'll be born there very soon;
Then, how that person that they see
Will measure up, it's up to me.

Verses 5,6,and 7 may be deleted.

© R. D. Carlin 1990

Richard   Carlin
Kennett   Square,   Pennsylvania,
USA

On top of this Burial Mound,
Surrounded by a landscape of trees,
A flaming cross burns
Fueled by the burning desire
Of each wildlife creature
That had not wanted to die -
Landscape architects bent over glossiness, flipped pages,
Selecting - costly - (time and expertise): Trees
To landscape the municipal cities' Burial Mound,
And for all to see like a billboard, there is an epitaph that reads:
'Within this Burial Mound, crushed forever into silence
Are the spirits of wildlife creatures whose voices had been mute
(As voices of wildlife creatures are heard by only a few).
The mass of techno-people had said,
"We don't have time; we're too busy to recycle,"
And with deftness of hands had tossed off into dumpsters:
Paper, glass, metal cans, plastic, tires, Styrofoam, food, plants, Xmas trees,
Never hearing the little hearts . . .
Beating in forests, beating in mountains, beating in rivers, lakes, oceans,
By the deftness of hands of habit of the techno-people
Tossing off solid waste, and were too busy to recycle.'
On top of this Burial Mound,
Surrounded by a landscape of trees,
A flaming cross burns
Fueled by the burning desire
Of each wildlife creature
That had not wanted to die -

Countess, Chairman
Palm Beach County Clean Sweep
P.O. Box 464
Palm Beach, Florida, USA

Save The Earth

Chorus:

Save the earth, it's our home you see.
Save the earth, make it clean and free.
Save the earth, come join with me.
Save the earth for posterity.

The time has come for all to hear
That 1990 is the year
For all the human race to pledge
To save our home for future kids.
We got a problem called pollution
All by ourselves there's no solution,
But if all the countries of the earth
Work together we'll give birth
To cleaner air and fresher water
Than any known by Mom and Father.
And we'll have less toxic matter
By watching how we buy and scatter
All the refuse of civilization.
We must come to the realization
That this ole planet just won't make it
Without our help to regenerate it.

Chorus

The jungles in the Amazon
Are looking like their neighbor's lawn.
The air's so thick with smoke and dust
I think my little lungs will bust.
A new species dies every minute
If you ask me we're lousy tenants.
We've got mountains of old rubber tires
The chemical companies are full of liars.
They say the waste from their little plants
Don't hurt any animals or plants
But just the noise is enough to scare
The eagles all away from there.
So if you're like me and want to see
A world of life and activity
Don't just pollute and waste and trash.
Conserve! Replant! Recycle trash!

Chorus

Tim Bosch
Box 89 Deep Meadow
Exeter, New Hampshire, USA
&
Jared Smith
21 Dartmouth Street
Exeter, New Hampshire, USA

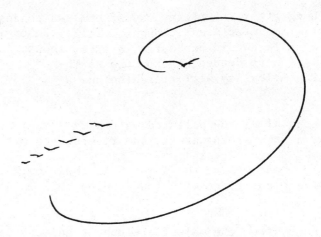

Marc   Siciliani
10458 1/2 Moorpark Street
Toluca Lake, California, USA

LOST EDEN

It chokes a sigh of concern,
With aging wounds, ever-aggravated,
Bleeding through the greenhouse roof.
The atmosphere is dying.

They burn with chemical fire,
Being raped of life and learning,
Defiled and left to die.
The seas are dying.

They fall like giants from wielded axe
Tumbling to the earth with mounting celerity;
These aged ancestors.
The forests are dying.

Eden, where has it gone?
God's good creation of this big blue marble
Has been neglected.
The curator of this garden paradise, ignoring their task.

Man ate the fruit which led
To greed and desire and ages since
Man has neglected, man has forgotten, rejected.
The earth is dying.

It's up to us ....

Derek   Albury
Nassau, Bahamas

Long after the milkey way of endless possessions..
        manufactured...bought...sold...belonging to,
        in untold cupboards, attics, shops, warehouses,
        have deadended into the earth-
The Milky Way will starshine on.

Long after the polluted waters..
        the groundwaters, the rivers, the wetlands, the dumped up oceans
        have rebelled,
        entangling the swimmer in their muck-
The great tides will continue to roll in and out.

Long after the majestic elephant and the spiritual dolphin
        and others we loved
        bid us fond adieu-
New life of unpredictable form will simmer in the cauldron of earth energy.

Long after the rainforests of Brazil, the forests of Indonesia and India,
        the venerable redwoods,
        invaded, decapitated, pulped,
        the spirits having fled-
The earth will gasp at the loss of its life-enhancers and convulse back.

Long after gases clog our breathing space
        and greed itself falls into the toxic abyss
        and ozone, greenhouse, acid rain are faded words in castoff memos-
The earth will weep with beneficent rain-
        Noah, how did you build that ark?

Long after Antartica
        the last refuge of pristine sanctity
        a symbol of space
                giving way to spirit
                        giving way to peace
                                giving way to unity of all life-
Little menlike birds with white shirt fronts and black flipper wings
        flutter and cry:

They didn't understand
They had it all
It was Paradise
The Earth

© Marlaina Kreinin 1990
1431 Sherwood Avenue
East Lansing, Michigan, USA

A smog covered ball of dust,
overcome by wishes and dreams
broken and dying,
lost,
in the rush of the world.

Cassandra Comstock
Ranger Robot Magazine, USA

I Have A Dream
That eagles fly over a clean Mother Earth
That animals have clean water to drink
And all the children in the world have enough to eat.

I Have A Dream
That dolphins and whales will be saved forever
And my ancestors' prayers and songs come true.

I Have A Dream
I will protect the Earth like a warrior,
And the Earth is safe as long as the bears live.

Craig Allen Magpie, Age 10
Cheyenne-Arapahoe
Santa Clara Day School
Santa Clara Pueblo
New Mexico, USA

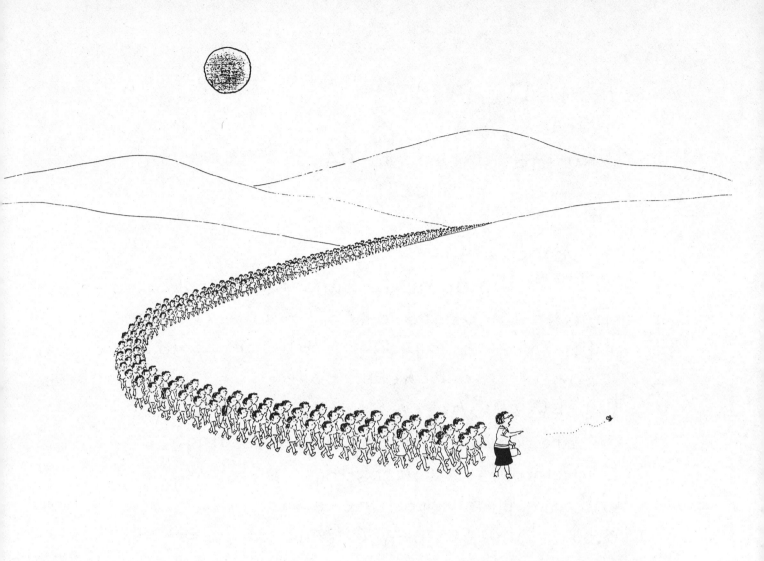

"The Last Butterfly"
George Brenner
Uj Ludas Mgz., Hungary

11. ... and the Young Shall Inherit ...?

Can a person read the letters of children and not remember what it was like to lie on the grass and watch the clouds slide across a summer sky? Is it possible for a person to immerse herself here among children's voices and not be taken back to the joys as well as the traumas of innocence? Is it conceivable that the game of success can so blind us, as adults, that in our determined rush for position and ease we risk our neighbors' children, and thereby our own as well? If what we feed them today will kill them tomorrow, what is the point? If the extra comforts we provide today will bring them extra hardships tomorrow, what is the gain? Our parents and grandparents, coming out of the Depression, were determined to make the world better for their children. Why aren't we making it better for ours? Who can hear the voices of the children and not feel shame?

Earth Day 1990
P.O Box, A A
Stanford University, CA
94309

Dear Sirs:
Hello, My name is Barbara Aubain.
I am 10 years old. I have brown
eyes and hair. I go to Springridge
Elem. My teacher's name is Miss
Moffett. She has blond, curley hair,
We are going to be studying ecology.
Our shcool is celebrating Earth Day.
Will you please send me some info.
about saving our planet. Thank you very
much.

Your friend,
Barbara Aubain

Barbara Jo Aubain
Springridge Elementary School
Richardson, Texas, USA

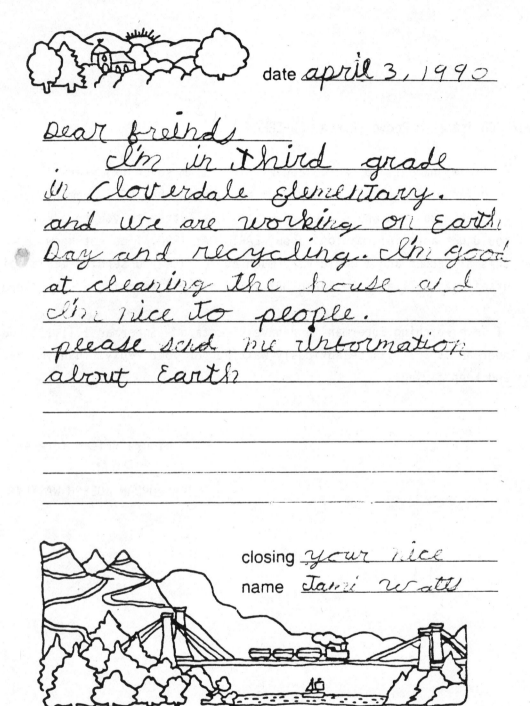

date april 3, 1990

Dear freinds

I'm in third grade
in Cloverdale elementary.
and we are working on Earth
Day and recycling. I'm good
at cleaning the house and
I'm nice to people.
please send me information
about Earth

closing your nice
name Tami Watts

Tami Watts
Cloverdale, Oregon, USA

Dear Christopher Reeve (A.K.A. SUPERMAN)

    Hello my name is Jordan Joseph Wasylyk, I am seven (7) years old. I
am a big fan of Superman . I saw your picture in the DC   comic book
called   FLASH 36 and would like to write this letter to you to ask
if I could get more information about EARTH DAY 1990. I do not know
what this all about and I would very much appreciate you sending me a picture
of yourself as well as the EARTH DAY info since I am doing a school project.

    I love watching Superman and have videotaped Superman I,II,III, but
not Superman IV . I will be anxiously waiting for your reply. Thankyou very
much and keep flying.

                                        Yours friend forever
                                        JORDAN
                                        JORDAN JOSEPH WASYLYK

                                        Jordan Joseph Wasylyk
                                        609 Gauthier Drive
                                        Tecumseh, Ontario, Canada

Dear Earth Day people

I need help. If I don't
get some big info on Earth Day
I will be devoured by my science
teacher. I need so much info
that I will get an A+ please
My life is in your hands

Lots of Info

Lots of Info

Lots of info

please
please
please
A+
A+
A+

Brock Walsh

Brock Walsh
Arlington, Virginia, USA

Earth Day week is the celebration of the earth. If we celebrate the earth we should make it a good place to live. What is earth without the environment? We should keep it clean. The pollutions are killing our world. The world is a beautiful planet, so if we destroy it, where would we live? Planet "earth" is the place where we could live because, the climate isn't too hot or cold. If you think of the world disappearing slowly infront of you're eyes, it is sad. We should cut down on the factories.

What can we do to help our environment?

Sincerely,
MyLe To
My Le To

MyLe To
Santa Clara, California, USA

Business Letter Form

1529 Mission Blvd,
Fayetteville, Ar.
72>0

Earth day 1990
National
Headquarters P.O
Box 44 Stanford,
Calif, 94309

Dear sir,

How are you doing? I'm
doing fine. I would like
free information and how
we can help. I do not
throw trach around. I
hope you don't eather.
Please write back. Thank
you.
Your friend,
Claire M.S.

Claire Michelle Smith
Fayetteville, Arkansas, USA

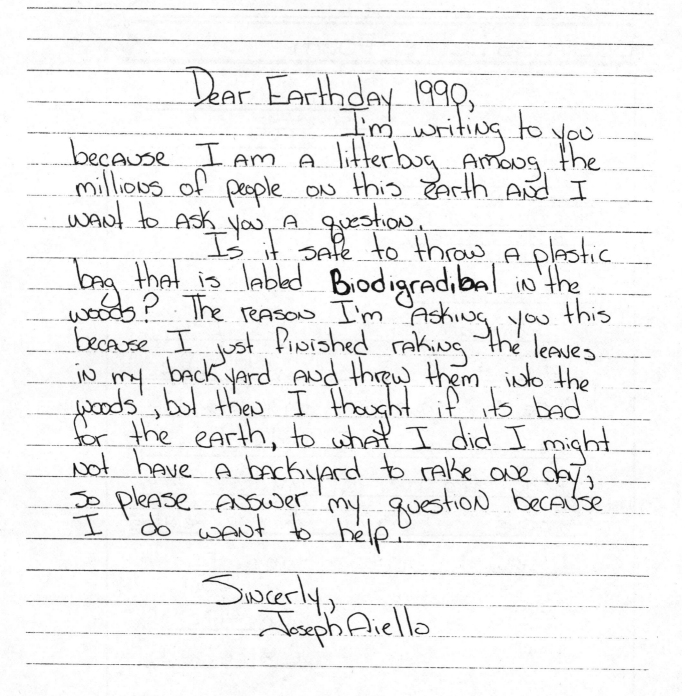

Dear Earthday 1990,
I'm writing to you because I am a litterbug among the millions of people on this earth and I want to ask you a question.

Is it safe to throw a plastic bag that is labled **Biodigradibal** in the woods? The reason I'm asking you this because I just finished raking the leaves in my backyard and threw them into the woods, but then I thought if its bad for the earth, to what I did I might not have a backyard to rake one day, so please answer my question because I do want to help.

Sincerly,
Joseph Aiello

Joseph Aiello
Ronkonkoma, New York, USA

FAIRFAX COUNTY
PUBLIC SCHOOLS

Bush Hill Elementary School
5927 Westchester Street
Alexandria, Virginia 22310

February 26, 1990

Dear Earth Day 1990,

We need information about Earth Day activities in the spring-field area close to Washington D.c. We want to know how to stop polluting the air. We want to know how to be good to our earth.

thank you,
Our First Grade class
Mrs. Robin McGirk

Andrew Connors   Andrew Postore   Jasneet Sandhu
Courtney Chapman   Jimmy Mickey   Haley Mustone
Stephanie wood   Stephen Fishel
                                     Adam Valeti
   Sherri Trollinger   Maria Gutierrez Gregory
Keir Myssen   Amanda Thomas   Gibson
   Ana Portilo   Jenny Delcid
              Daeyang Connery
              Kristin Peavely

Robin McGirk's First Grade Class: Courtney Chapman, Daeyang Connery, Andrew Connors, Jenny Delcid, Stephan Fishel, Gregory Gibson, Maria Gutierrez, Jimmy Mickey, Keir Mussen, Haley Mustone, Andrew Pastore, Kristin Peavely, Ana Portillo, Jasneet Sandhu, Amanda Thomas, Sherri Trollinger, Adam Valenti, Stephanie Wood
Bush Hill Elementary School
5927 Westchester Street
Alexandria, Virginia, USA

2   3-8-90

Dear Sir,

    We need a clean earth. If we have dirty air, everybody will die. I have asthma, so if I breath dirty air, my lungs will turn black and I will sick. Please send us some more information.

              Sincerly,

       Benjamin D. Barnett

Benjamin D. Barnett
Irving, Texas, USA

Me llamo laura Maria Gutierrez Escobar estudio en el colegio Jose Juaquin Castro Martinez, en el grado cuarto.

Tengo nueve años y medio y estoy aprendiendo ingles con clases en mi casa.

La primera clase fue el sabado pasado.

Siento mucho no poderles escribirles en ingles pero talves el prooximo año si.

Voy a tratar de colaborar todos lo años en esa Fiesta tan importante porque tal vez los elefantes y muchos animales mas nuestros hijos no podran conocerlos.

Los sistemas Bioticos.

Una Laguna.

Un rio.

El Bosque

Estos sistemas Bioticos todavia algunos no estan contaminados como muy pocos rios. hojala que no siga asi ¡Hay que sembrar y ayudar! a la conservacion de la natura

Laura Maria Gutierrez Escobar
Jose Juaquin Castro School

I used to think it sounded like a cliche, but we (the young people) are really the future of the world. And we've got to do all we can to save this beautiful planet, 'cause frankly, it's the only home we've got. It's about time people start giving something back to the Earth Mother, instead of just take, take, taking all the time!

Lorraine Marie Fisher "Gypsy"
5829 Hosac Way
Citrus Heights, California, USA

I really like earth Day. It is the best holiday. Would you please send me a baby tree. But the only thing bad about having a tree, I live in apartment but I can do it in a pot. And would you please write back to me.

Jonathan   Pichardo
Boca Raton. Florida, USA

My name is Cory Lambert and I would like to tell you a few things. I would like you to get the lead out please. I would like to see a few things done. Our earth is slowly deteriorating. Sometimes I think you are not doing your job. George Bush said that he was going to start up a group to clean up the earth, but no one did anything. I sure am glad that Michael Dukakis didn't become president. He could have done for us what he has done for Mass. I'm not telling you how to do your job, I would just like to see something done.

Cory   Lambert
Monticello, Iowa, USA

People, People, you should be 'shame', 'cause look at our planet, so dirty and full of trash. Did you know that the ozone layer is dying because of us? That's bad because our planet's dying and when our planet dies we die too. So there's something to think about. You must think it's too late. Well, it's not. If you recycle garbage we could save our planet. And if we get together we could do it like on Earth Day. Everybody get together from north to south, from east to west. So, come on people, recycle your cans and recycle your paper. Ride a bike so you can't pollute the air. Please help.

USA

Dear Earth Day,

The thing that concern's me the most is the trees. The trees shouldn't be cut down because some animals need to live there. Also if they cut down the trees the forest would look empty, and there would be just dirt. If the animals stay there they can easily be killed by the hunters.

Thanks for your time!

From
Ruth Popa

Ruth Popa

Ruth Popa
North Royalton, Ohio, USA

Hi. My name Olivia Van Wye. I am 10 years old. My family is very nice. Just the other night at 10:00 I shut the door on my sister's finger, but I didn't mean to.

My teacher's name is Julie Moffett. She is very nice. I bet you all would like her. My principal's name is Ann Adams. She is nice also. Please send information.

Olivia Van Wye
Richardson, Texas, USA

Karen D. H. Warden
Lawrence, Kansas, USA

12. *To a new consciousness awakening!*

Scott Crawford
890 Broadway
Somerville, Massachusetts, USA

Following the publication of an article about Earth Day in "NEA Today", fully 75% of the mail came from educators. Over the whole campaign, the most represented group was Elementary and Pre-school teachers. Theirs were mostly brief letters-- requests for lesson plans, information, and activities. Probably short on time, and definitely short on resources (see Chapter 6), they were, and are, fully engaged in *the essential* occupation of a healthy democracy: the processes of forming good people. When education makes people aware, they tend to take the right actions; they tend to consider the whole instead of just their own needs. Their example teaches others, and the circle expands. Thus, teachers are the key activists in this rapidly growing movement

There is some question about what it means to be an 'activist'. As one letter declared, "I want to get involved, as long as I don't have to protest . . ." Yet, many of the fine qualities of our nation were achieved through actions by activists. Activists threw the tea into the Boston Harbor, demonstrated for equal rights, marched for women's suffrage, and protested the Viet Nam War. Activists were instrumental recently in dismantling the cold war arsenals.

Usually activism has meant being against someone, or against a social or political institution. Unless one demonstrated publicly, one's private views on the issue at hand had no political power. But activism can also be positive. Through our conscious actions we can begin to clean up the mess which our unconscious actions caused. In the environmental movement, actions do not have to be taken *against*; actions can be taken *for*. This chapter is about solutions.

I am very concerned with what is happening to our world. Sometimes I think about what our world will be like when I'm older. Will people have come together to clean up our world with clean air and water, or will people be laid back not caring about our environment. . . What I think is scary is that we are hurting ourselves and it can be helped.

Jamie Manganello
16846 Leroy Avenue
Los Gatos, California, USA

Earth Day 1990 is now past and gone, but here at ACSDI we are always trying to answer the question: Are we doing enough? And, are we fast enough to save Mother Earth? Can we make the necessary quantum leap forward in our thinking to work TOGETHER AS ONE MASS OF HUMANITY? We are optimistic that the survivalist instinct of man, if not his spirituality, will nudge him to make the necessary 'open-minded' decisions and actions to save Mother Earth.

Ogunseitan O'seun
African Center for Science and
Development
Lagos, Nigeria

I saw a wonderful article on Earth Day in Rolling Stone Magazine. I am thirteen years old and as of yet have never been presented with an opportunity to become an activist. I believe I would like nothing better than to carry out the orders of the veteran nineteen sixties and seventies activists who I am sorry I could not be among from the beginning.

Michael   Klinger
White Plains, New York, USA

Activity/Passivity

Aktivitet   Passivitet

Stefan   Hansson
ISU AB, Sweden

I'm tired of saying that "I'll get involved," when I never do. It's time we all realized that we <u>have</u> to get involved <u>NOW</u> or we won't have a world to live in!

Lisa   Wingert
Cleveland, Ohio, USA

Science classes wrote letters to two cruise ship lines known to release helium balloons to celebrate trip departures. They were informed (quite eloquently!) of the danger of this practice to land and sea animals.

USA

We are a third grade class at the Carpenter School in Chicago, Illinois. We know how important it is to take care of the earth. We recycle and have collected $1,000. We donated it to the Lincoln Park Zoo for the endangered Spectacled Bears.

Anthony Redisi
617 North Racine Avenue
Chicago, Illinois, USA

The KaNgwane Parks Corporation believes that conservation should benefit people in the short term as well as in the future. This is particularly so in KaNgwane where many people lack even the basic needs of a reliable water supply, fuel, and shelter . . . therefore, (we try) to utilize for conservation land which has a poor agricultural potential. This land will often yield more if it is developed as a game reserve. At present the Corporation has five reserves . . .

Karl Lane
KaNgwant Parks Corporation
Nelsprit, South Africa

I see a real need to reach out and educate our children on the responsibilities of our quick demand lifestyles vs. the environmental outcomes. I see many kids escape into the world of video games vs. escaping into the world of the outdoors.

Pamela S. Beltz,
Cacapon State Park
Berkeley Springs, West Virginia, USA

One of my scouts, Keith DiGregory, developed an Eagel Scout project which was to plant 300 trees along the shoreline on the north shore of Long Island. This project has been fulfilled as of April 14, 1990. Now he is in the process of caring for these seedlings and watching that their growth continues to maturity.

Joseph Jacobs
Asst. Scoutmaster - Troop 161
Ridge, New York, USA

The Dutch Friends of the Earth, the Foundation for Nature and Environment, the Dutch Bicycle Association and others are planning a large demonstration against the growth of traffic and highways in Holland . . . Trees will be planted on the spot the government is planning a new (superfluous) highway.

Holland.

I have planted over 400 trees, as well as bushes and flowers, in my back yard (a city lot); and I'm still planting! My aim: to create a miniforest. When I bought the property, the land had been stripped of trees.

Dorothy Dabney Kehoe
921 W. 18th Avenue
Covington, Louisiana, USA

We are planning to plant more than 1,500,000 trees and we will use churches, primary schools, high schools, and local people in the area.
May the lord almighty be with you till we communicate with you again.

Reverend. T.O. Nyokeya
Evangelical Fellowship of Kenya
Homa Bay, Kenya

In October, 1988, Hurricane Joan leveled Bluefields, a major port on the Atlantic coast of Nicaragua. Winds up to 180 miles per hour beat at the city for twelve hours. Almost all the wildlife in the region was killed, and at least one-half million acres of tropical rainforest was destroyed.

April 22nd will truly be Earth Day in the Caribbean city of Bluefields, Nicaragua, as forty young people from the United States, the Soviet Union, Costa Rica, and Nicaragua finish a two-week project planting thousands of fruit trees in (the) devastated area.

The PeaceTrees Nicaragua initiative is coordinated by the Earthstewards Network, a citizen . . . organization based on Bainbridge Island, Washington. The work in Nicaragua comes after similar efforts in Costa Rica and India and will be followed by three Urban PeaceTrees efforts in which young people from the Soviet Union, Costa Rica, India, and Northern Ireland will join U.S. counterparts to plant trees in the inner cities of Washington, DC, Los Angeles, and New York.

At some point in the 1990's, I believe we will see thousands of young people from our . . . nations working together each year in the Soviet Union and the United States and the so-called 'developing' nations to address the pressing ecological challenges before us. The only arms we can afford to give the warriors of the 21st century are their own, to plant trees and dig wells and construct solar homes.

Dwight Wilson
Earthstewards Network
P.O. Box 10697
Winslow, Washington, USA

The Programme for Belize, formed in 1988, is a consortium of international organizations including the Audubon Society, World Wildlife Fund, Nature Conservancy, and others. The main goal of Programme for Belize is to respond to an invitation by the Belizan Government to participate directly in the effort to link development and conservation in ways that advance the objectives of both. Currently, the Programme for Belize has a goal of raising enough money to preserve 42,000 acres of forest, savannah, and wetlands. Each $50 raised will secure one acre.

Rainforest Run
3860 Chippewa Court
San Diego, California, USA

All the science classes in 7th grade are trying to make a difference, we are trying to get our school to recycle paper, plastic, and styrofoam dishes that are in the cafeteria. We recently went to a local board meeting and stated how we would like to boycott tuna which kills dolphins. We are also looking for other things to do to improve our environment, and I'm sure we'll find ways. The kids at Lincoln School are trying to make a difference for our future!

Sara Jones
32 Mercury Lane
Jamestown, New York, USA

P.S. We also got in the paper for going to the board meeting on boycotting tuna.

In our school . . . we have a club called the "Clean-up Club" and we pick up trash around our school. There are 16 members in the Clean-up Club . . . 3 people go out at recess each day to collect the trash.

Megan Householder & Elizabeth Parker
Westerly School
30301 Wolf Road
Bay Village, Ohio, USA

I'm from Vermont where we grew up with Green Day . . . we got out of school for the day and picked up garbage around the cities . . .

Ami Ayne Wennar
Washington, D.C., USA

I'm not real faithful in protecting our environment, but I would like more information on how I could be. A person is never totally aware of all things he could be doing, but it would be nice if we were more informed. That is what I would like to be, more informed . . .

Mrs. Sperry
Rt. 3 Box 119
Montevideo, Minnesota, USA

I have learned in my science class some facts, such as it takes more than 500,000 trees to produce all the newspapers Americans read in one Sunday. Did you know that every 20 minutes Americans dump enough cars into junk yards to form a stack as high as the Empire State Building? O, well, thanks for your time.

Willie Kolarik
Hutchinson Junior High (Sci 205)
3102 Canton
Lubbock, Texas, USA

One idea that occurred to me as I read OMNI's special issue dedicated to the environment was to print out flyers of facts, such as
. . . for each ton of paper recycled, 3,700 pounds of lumber and 24,000 gallons of water are saved.
. . . 5,000 Northern Fur Seals are drowned each year by plastic fishing nets.

USA

I'm a 12 year old girl . . . At the beginning of the year I did not know much on the topic; I did not know just how much our world was in danger. As we learned more and more of these difficulties . . . I began to worry--it began to get scary--but that's what also made me take more action in the matter. There are so many problems and so few solutions.

Nita K. Mangat
Everett, Washington, USA

My little Katie is only seven months old, so maybe it seems silly for me to begin educating her about her environment. But maybe, just maybe, if I can instill in her a love for her home (by that I mean the planet) she will be one more person who will not stand for or put up with the evil crimes continually committed against this earth.

Michele and Katie Paulsen
USA

I participated in the first Earth Day in 1970 and the experience helped me to become a lifetime conservationist. If we can teach children at an early age to respect the environment this will have a lasting effect on the planet.

Roger E. Fitzgerald
Hampstead, Maryland, USA

I feel it is imperative to instill in each child the desire to try to make the world of today a better place in which to live, so that there will indeed be a world of tomorrow . . . To that end I am stressing environmental awareness in all my groups. Together we can change the seemingly bleak outlook of our world.

Mrs. Judy Lowrey, XTAR
Xenia City Schools
578 E. Main Street
Xenia, Ohio, USA

Please send as quickly as possible your information packet on Earth Day. I have been sick with cancer and am just able to get back to the classroom. Much to my dismay, Earth Day is closer than I thought.

Cindy McReynolds
Story School
Loop 256
Palestine, Texas, USA

I teach kindergarten and . . . I want my students to have the mind set they can change the world!

USA

"The world's sustained by the breath of children learning."

The Talmud
Solomon Schechter Day School
St. Louis, Missouri, USA

Enclosed is my modest contribution.

In 1970, on April 22, when the first Earth Day was celebrated, I was a coordinator for the program that took place at the University of New Hampshire. It was a wonderful event and involved hundreds of people; and a lot of workshops; seminars; retreats; guest speakers (including Ralph Nader; Stewart Udall; John Kerry;)and others.

Unfortunately, Earth Day on April 22, 1970 was a failure. We did all the good things; we protested; we were self-righteous; we told the world we had the answers; and we were sincere. On reflection, we really were true believers.

When April 22, 1970, came and went, those who took part and made a contribution, returned to their former styles. In a way, we seemed to recognize the problem; perhaps we accepted the fact that we were part of the problem; but the 1970 crowd of Earth Day advocates, on the whole, did little but wear buttons; talk in platitudes; promise to change things; express anger and outrage at the authorities and the institutions; and,when it was over, most of us congratulated ourselves on our accomplishments and dutifully returned to our former ways. Nothing much changed.

Earth Day 1990 offers another opportunity and a greater challenge. For me, it will involve teaching and telling the youngsters at Strafford Elementary School about their earth. They do not know what's happening; they don't know how perilously close we all are to extinction; they will not understand even if I tell them. And so I will not talk about this to them.

I think what I will do is to tell them and show them how they are a part of the earth. I'll try to tell them that everything they do will make a difference. And, in my own way, I will try to give them a good example.

Ray Matheson

Ray Matheson, Teacher
Strafford Elementary and Middle School
Center Strafford, New Hampshire, USA

Hello! My name is Neha Majumdar and I am an eighteen year old senior in high school . . . Two weeks ago I was in New Orleans and I stopped by the Earth Day booth at the zoo. This was the first time I was exposed to your organization. One of the volunteers spoke with me about half an hour and I decided it was time for me to stop sitting on my bottom watching other people clean up the environment I am a part of. I guess until speaking with the volunteers I never thought about environmental problems and how dangerous things are becoming. Well, now I know and I want to make a commitment to help any way possible.

Neja Majumdar
Niles, Illinois, USA

Earth Day is the greatest day for me; I believe everyday is Earth Day. Michelle and I (Jimmy) have been trying very hard to keep the area in which we live as clean as possible. But it seems so hard. Everyday as we walk to work--or anywhere we walk--we pick up cans to recycle and pick up trash and place it in the nearest garbage cans. We have no car and we plan on getting bikes instead of cars. When we need to go someplace that is a distance too far to walk or ride a bike, we ride the bus.

We live in Houston, Texas. My girlfriend, Michelle, and I plan on being married soon. We've been together for six months now. She's 18 and I'm 21. As I was watching the special that was on T.V. tonight, I started to cry. I know that probably sounds stupid, but I really feel worried and scared.

I also need some information on things that are recyclable, and where I can send funds to help out as much as possible. We could use the money we make from recycling as funds for the rainforest, preserving our oceans, and whatever else . . .

I hope someone really reads this and responds. I and my girlfriend really want to do our part, for our future and our children when we have them.

Love and Sincerity,

Jimmy and Michelle Bryant
622 Janisch
Houston, Texas, USA

Hi! I am 15 yrs. old & I want to make a difference!!! My parents say "people need to make their kids start considering what's been going on in this world & to take action!" Most kids parents worry their kids with grades in school & stuff like that, and grades are important, but if we don't act NOW there aren't going to be any grades to worry about.

USA.

Our 10 year old son, Scott, has really enlightened our family on how important it is to "save the earth." His school, Lessenger Elementary School, has initiated many projects and learning programs to recycle. Our family (now) recycles bottles, cans, and plastic containers, and disposes of oil and batteries properly. Also, we try to use safe-for-the-environment products.

Pat Sanford
856 W. 13 Mile Road
Madison Heights, Michigan, USA

I have recently become interested in saving the earth from destruction. Everything I do, whether it be flushing the toilet or throwing away a piece of paper, I think about what will happen to it. Also, my family has switched to many organic and recyclable products . . .

Angela Kiddoo
4614 47th Street
Moline, Illinois, USA

Just recently I started to become more aware of our resources and how important they really are. I started turning lights off when they aren't in use, recycling paper and glass . . . yet it still doesn't seem like I'm doing enough.

Bonnie Hayes Cox
Edenton, North Carolina, USA

I remember just a year ago how helpless I felt when I first became aware of the great environmental injustices that man was doing to his world. At that time, it seemed to me that no one cared; they couldn't be bothered with such petty things as deforestation, CFC's, or dolphins dying for the sake of a tunafish sandwich.

Since then however, I've been getting Greenpeace Magazine, I've joined an environmental awareness group at school, and gone to protests. I'm seeing now that there are people who really do care, and believe me, it feels good.

The environmental movement is growing; it's gaining ground; and it's terrific!

Michael Lundie
November Lane
Plantsville, Connecticut, USA

At 78, having for many years been an advocate of Natural Food, Natural Healing, and Natural Living, in the days when the mere mention of these ideals evoked scorn and ridicule, I am excited over this new Era of Enlightenment.

Arthur Jackson
37 Watkins Road
Brick, New Jersey, USA

I'm really "fired up." I'm a veteran of the 1970 Earth Day and I want to give my kindergarten students and their families the fever too!

Lynn Raasch
4171 Fairview Road
Greenwood, Indiana, USA

I truly feel that this movement will continue to snowball, and we can and will make a difference!

Maria Heller
540 West Penn Street
Long Beach, New York, USA

18 January 1990

Dear Earthday 90 Group,

I'm really glad you're bringing it back. Where can we get buttons? Bumper stickers? Earth Day 90! Earth Day II!

After "Earth Day", year one, every day's seemed like Earth Day to me: it's a kind of holiday y' can have everyday. Earth Day 90: 7,300 earthdays celebrated since "Earth Day."

My first Earth Day, I was walking along Green Street, Delaware, Ohio. Green Street's off Main Street; I was a few blocks from downtown--the movie theatre, drug store, bookstores, and a liberal arts college. I was into my second year there.

It was spring; afternoon. It seemed like all the school and all the town was out walking the streets together, neighborhood groups, fraternity groups, dormitory groups, girl scout groups, hippie groups, other family groups; individuals with a backpack, paper-sack, book-bag, or a wagon, just strollin' along, pickin' up trash.

The next day there'd be newspaper photos of people in the riverside shallows holding up tin cans.

All around the country there were photos of people up to their knees in a river, holding up trash high overhead.

. . .

The last Earth Day for me, see, was yesterday, when I picked up somebody else's mcburger-wrapper. Didn't take much effort. I used t'get sore, but I don't anymore. Figure it's worth it--easy--to make that little effort to keep the world lookin' good.

I'm looking forward to Earth Day 90 as a happy celebration of a good phrase, and of the public recognition that we, every one of all of us, are in it together . . . and "it" is piled higher every day, and every day is Earth Day: it ought to be; it's go t t'be!

Matt Levin
Hatfield, Massachusetts, USA

I am ten and I am concerned about our environment. I believe that we are destroying it to such an extent that there will soon be very little left. But I also believe that I myself can do something about it.

Tiffany Stoddard
Dublin, Ohio, USA

I am a sixth grade teacher and . . . I know one person can make a difference. I also know that a hundred students and their families can make a bigger difference.

Marilyn Grubbs
431 West Ansley
San Antonio, Texas, USA

In 1984, Barbara Hubert's 8th graders in Wichita, Kansas wanted to make the world better. "We could help plant fruit trees in poor countries," said one student. "Yeah," another said, "fruit has vitamins and trees are good for the soil and air." With a car wash they earned enough to plant 103 fruit trees in a village in India. Since then, Trees for Life has planted 3 million fruit and forest trees in many countries. Each fruit tree will produce thousands of pounds of fruit during its lifetime and help fight pollution.

Proceeds . . . will be used by Trees for Life to fund tree-planting kits for school children and to help meet the Trees for Life goal of planting 100 million fruit trees for food and fuel in developing countries throughout the world in the 90's. . . . by banding together, each one of us can make a difference . . .

Margalee Wright & Jim Callaway
Trees for Life
1103 Jefferson
Wichita, Kansas, USA

If we could join together all across America and around the world, think of all the good we could do.

Sunny Cava, Seventh Grade
5027 Elester Drive
San Jose, California, USA

In my house, the simplest things have become fraught with significance of late. Take laundry. It was a straightforward matter, once upon a time. The hamper got full and I did the wash. Now every aspect of this routine chore is subject to intense scrutiny.

For years I dutifully plonked down my contributions to the big environmental groups. I was heartsick over the environment, and I didn't know what else to do. Then along came Earth Day . . . it was the nudge I needed. Earth Day didn't convert me from indifference to true belief--I was a believer already-- but rather from sympathy to activism.

We earth-lovers are not just another special-interest group. We are prophets, would-be transformers of the world. We are not seeking merely a new law or a new program, but a new vision to guide us: a world order based on love and gentleness toward Creation. And we want a way of life that is consonant with our beliefs. For the devout, writing checks can never be enough.

I know it seems silly--maybe even sacrilegious, to some--to discuss laundry and light bulbs in such terms. To most people, laundry is morally neutral. . . But . . . like all religious rituals, the importance of these acts lies not so much in their effect on society as in their role in the life of the believer.

Hanging out laundry--as ludicrous as it seems--is an act of faith. Each time I put a diaper out to dry, I reaffirm my belief. In a hundred tiny acts each day, I renew my commitment to preserve the world and its inhabitants.

Perhaps it wasn't Earth Day that changed me. Perhaps it was the Earth herself.. For how else can I explain it? I like hanging out the clothes. The rhythm is gentle. The sun is warm. An oriole sings. . . My insignificant act has made Nature immediate and real . . . I slow down a moment, to drink it all in. If you promise not to laugh this time, I'll tell you what I believe: that it is Gaia, the earth goddess, herself, whispering in my ear, encouraging me, bringing me softly into alignment with her most wondrous self.

"Saving the Earth Through Laundry"
Elizabeth Feuer
The New York Times
April 22, 1990

I am thrilled with the coming of Earth Day 1990 and the dawning of a new consciousness.

Paige Miller
Durango, Colorado, USA

(The first two pages of this letter were lost.)

them. It is this attitude towards nature that may save us and make
the sky blue again and the meadows and forests green. Only this
kind of feeling may wash the clouds clean and return the long-
-forgotten fresh look to our cities and make the grass smell of joy
again and the water bring life.

We beleive there will come a time when the nations will be proud
not of their factories and smoggy horizons, but of green leaves,
the dews and the coolness of nights and of the scent of their mists
and marshlands.

We beleive that schoolchildren will be learning to write: the
air is our father. The water is the mother. The Earth is our home.
The dew is the national treasure.

Igor Shklyarevsky
chairman of the ecological movement "The Eyes of
the Earth"

D.S.Likhachev
academician, chairman of the Soviet Culture Fund

Genrikh Borovik
chairman of the Soviet Peace Committee

Boris Oleynik
Deputy Chairman of the Soviet of Nationalities of the Supreme Soviet
of the USSR

Miroslav Barvircak
Czechoslovakia

POSTSCRIPT

Earth Day is a campaign not to clean up the environment but to establish worldwide control: control over the environment, control over the people, control over everything.

Bessie M. Barnebee
2318 S. Vassar Road
Burton, Michigan, USA

From a small, rag-tag band of enthusiastic environmentalists occupying far too much office space, Earth Day grew to a full scale campaign squeezed by the walls. At its height, 2000 pieces of mail and 1600 phone calls came in every day. But within two weeks after the April 22 event, the 40 full-time staff members and 800 local volunteers had shrunk to four people. Control and power were not the ambitions of Earth Day 1990. Instead, it was communication. Did it succeed? or was it just a "flash in the pan", a show, a fad soon to be dropped and forgotten?

. . . you should know I'm not very optimistic about the future of our earth. I wish I could be. I'm almost 60. I won't be around in 2010. I fear for the youngsters who are now 12, and 13, and 14. I, and my generation, have made a mess of it. We didn't pay attention. We looked out for ourselves and didn't think about the consequences for the youngsters who would follow us. I cry about this, often.

My fond hope is that 2010 will not be a repeat of 1970 and 1990. Each time, we seem to have waited 20 years to recognize we are in trouble. Each time we do things that express our anger; each time we promise to do something; but each time we take only half steps. The time is ripe for us to take full steps!

Ray Matheson, Teacher
Strafford Elem./Middle School,
Center Strafford
New Hampshire, USA

Earth Day 1990 has passed. Seeds of environmental concern which lay dormant before April 22, 1990 have germinated. Neither the thunder nor the clouds of the Earth Day campaign can make things grow, but "water" from Earth Day's media campaign has soaked in, and already sprouts appear. In a few years the environmental movement, which now looks more like a desert, will then look more like a forest. Earth Day, not the organization, nor the staff who put it together, nor the volunteers who made it happen, but the day itself, the celebration of Life, the giving of thanks for every beast, for the pulse which whispers even in the last and most primative plant, will inspire and nurture Humankind far into the future. Earth Day is there to serve, as the rain serves.

Late this morning, as I was riding back home from Cavite, I was reading about the Blue Tit Warbler of Europe and the Macaca Fuscata monkey of Japan. The author was relating how . . . once the Blue Tit Warbler discovered how to open the foil caps of milk bottles left on doorsteps and to drink off the top cream, and once Blue Tits in one small area had taught each other this trick, suddenly all the other Blue Tits across the entire European continent were doing the same thing! So, too, after the Macaca Muscata monkeys on one island discovered how to wash freshly dug sweet potatoes, and once they taught this to other monkeys on the island, suddenly all the other monkeys of that species on other islands and even on the mainland were doing it too!

It occurs to me that somehow this is an apt description of what we are trying to do now--painstakingly but joyfully trying to hasten the approach of this threshold of change for the betterment of our Planet, and the realization of our common vision . . . For me, the Letters to Earth Day is another demonstration that small as the Blue Tit warbler may be, its song continues to be heard across the continents. So, too, will our Letters.

To our common hopes.

Elin B. Mondejar
Southeast Asia Regional
Institute for Community
Education
P.O. Box EA - 31 Ermita
Manila, Philippines

Dear Earth day

I recycle, plant trees and make compost heaps. I do all I can.

Your friend,
Andy Johnson

Andy Johnson
360 Tusculum Road
Nashville, Tennessee, USA

Addendum:

"The Isthmus of Karelia"
by Serge Tsvetkov

The Lake Region in trouble
A Proposal for Establishing the Isthmus of Karelia National Park

For many years there have been discussions in Leningrad about creating a National Park in the Isthmus of Karelia. This area is unique in many respects. On the west it borders on the Gulf of Finland, and on the east the great Lake Ladoga. This wedge of land, with its point resting on Leningrad and its top serving as the border with Finland, is divided by two massive geologic structures: the Baltic crystalline shield, and the Russian platform. The territory has come under attack four times by glaciers, leaving numerous tracks and a unique, diverse natural setting.

Canoers make good use of the Vucksa passage, consisting of hundreds of large and small lakes stretching from north to south along the glacier's track, joined by numerous rivers and streams. This magnificent system is joined with the Saimaa lake region situated in Finish territory and ending at the confluence of the Vuoksa River with Lake Ladoga. The waters of this region have always been famed for their crystal clarity and their abundance of cold water fish such as trout and salmon. The rocky northern portion of the Isthmus is framed on on the east and west by Lake Ladoga and the Gulf of Finland, and is dotted with picturesque mountains, long time favorites of rick climbers. On the cliffs not far from the village of Kuznechnoye, national rock climbing competitions have been held.

Toward the south, the major features of the Isthmus have been defined by rocky ridges and former moraines, containing pearl-like lakes left by the long gone glaciers. They are reminiscent of railroad embankments stretching out for dozens of kilometers.

Well proportioned and tidy pine forests impart a magnificent originality to this lake region. Numerous varieties of berries and mushrooms are found in the Isthmus' forests. As well, elk, hare, fox, wolves, waterfowl, and game are found in abundance.

This fairytale region now finds itself under constant threat of annihilation. The Svetogorsk pulp and paper combine contributes its fumes and wastes. The Kamennogorsk paper factory discharges its wastes into the crystal clear waters of the Vuoksa without any purification. In the village of Kamennogorsk, West German equipment has already been delivered for a factory which will produce formic acid in spite of the government prohibition against constructing new industrial enterprises in the Lake Ladoga watershed (which now hardly copes with the pollution it receives). Can you imagine what awaits Lake Ladoga when they throw this at it? In the numerous rock quarries one can hear the dynamite as they mine rock for construction uses. Many quarries have been abandoned and numerous lakes have been destroyed by gravel production. The water of the Vuoska is covered with rainbows from the oil sheen, and crude oil can be found along the shores.

Neighboring Finland adds its share to the cocktail of pollution. Our neighbor knows very well the testing schedule of the Soviet environmental protection workers and tried to discharge pollutants during the testing intervals, forgetting that the pollutants eventually

182

return: once discharged to the Vuoksa, the pollutants flow to Lake Ladoga, then on to the Neva River, and then to the Gulf of Finland and to Finland's own shores. So, like a boomerang, much of the pollution that we may think we have long since gotten rid of returns to us. This is all reminiscent of a story described by Jerome K. Jerome in his book "Three in a boat, not counting the dog' in which the hero could not rid himself of some ripe Dutch cheese. However, in contrast with this humorous story, ours is not so funny.

Much of the forest has ben cut on the Isthmus of Karelia and when the logs are floated down the rivers many end up on the bottom in a rotting boardwalk which has all but wiped out the salmon spawning grounds. Also, the land reclamation work in the central part of the Isthmus, where the rivers and streams are nourished, threatens to destroy them.

Not long ago in the USSR they began allotting land to city dwellers for garden plots. They did not omit the Isthmus of Karelia. Instead of using the less ecologically valuable land, they began the indiscriminate destruction of first rate forests. On the balding shores of the previously picturesque lakes, villages of dachas are suddenly appearing. They are sometimes built right on the edge of the lakes in the violation of our laws, and the surrounding forests are becoming cluttered with garbage dumps.

I remember the campaign to save the unique Lake Tyenuksenyarvi situated in the Tosnyensky hills. The military bureaucracy decided to build a dacha village on its shores. The protests of the local residents, the activists and ecologists, the reports in the press and on television, the fact that the lake was amonument of Nature, and even the intervention of the government environmental inspectors did not help. The all powerful military just declared the area a prohibited zone and quickly cut down all the trees along the shore. Amazingly, the dacha residents themselves did not understand how quickly they could turn this clear lake water to poison with their own pollution. This is an excellent example of just how far we are from a harmonious existence with Nature. The great desire is to possess a dainty tidbit, without any thought of the future.

There are many such happenings on the Isthmus of Karelia. The chairman of the Leningrad Regional Land Commission of the Council of Peoples Deputies, Korotov, has generously handed out dacha plots right and left in this unique Isthmus territory, particularly to Party functionaries and to bureaucrats. And all this was done in the name of caring for the people.

I know of only one instance where a land allotment for dacha plots was stopped. Paradoxically, this was accomplished by children. They stood in the path of the bulldozers which were uprooting trees near Zerkalnoye (Mirror) Lake. The workers immediately took the side of the children and stopped work. Information came out in the press that this plot of ground was earmarked for an upper manager, and this barbarous destruction of Nature was stopped. But this example, I repeat, was the only one.

This mindless annihilation of a unique corner of our planet can only be stopped by creating a national park in the Isthmus of Karelia. It is appropriate to remember that fifty years ago this land belonged to Finland. Full realization would be to create a Soviet-Finish National Park on the Isthmus of Karelia. The entrance to the park would have to be open to both sides. On the Isthmus of Karelia there are numerous abandoned Finnish farms which ought to be restored. They not only could give shelter to visitors, but they could also give a picture of peasant life in a former time.

However, before the National Park can be given full-blooded life, it is necessary, at a minimum, to declare the Isthmus a reserve. One must not forget about the precarious ecological condition of Lake Ladoga, the partitioning of the Gulf of Finland with the dam, a portion of which, the so-called Neva mouth, has been converted to a cesspool of sewage from a city of five million. As a result of this criminal dam construction (ostensibly to protect Leningrad from flooding), there has been a sharp deterioration of the ecological conditions in the eastern portion of the gulf of Finland. The resort areas along the shore are now subjected to a flow of polluted water directed at them by the dam's sluice-gate structures. As a result, the incidence of meningitis and intestinal infection has increased, particularly among children who have swum in the Gulf. Sixty percent of all water samples contain pathogenic bacteria. The water is now recognized as being epidemiologically dangerous. In regards to Lake Ladoga, the volume of all the tributary rivers and streams is hardly sufficient to dilute the pollutants . . . and this lake is the drinking cup of the five million Leningraders.

I think that creation of the National Park would serve as a stimulus for solving the ecological problems of the entire Leningrad region. One certainly cannot enjoy Nature if it is bordered on two sides by poisonous waters. It is utopian to hope for the revival of the Lake Region if the Leningrad enterprises do not stop discharging their wastes to the Gulf of Finland without purification, and if the dam remains.

Recently, the Commission of the Academy of Sciences of the USSR, on which I served, completed an examination of the Leningrad dam project. The Commission submitted their decision that the dam construction should be stopped, and two alternative solutions should be analyzed: either completely dismantle the dam, or convert it to a bridge with locks that can be closed in the event of a flood. But in order for the decision of the academic Commission to become a decision of the government, it will take a large effort of the city populace. I am certain that the creation of a National Park would, in many ways, speed the solution of this problem.

I very much hope that the idea of the creation of an Isthmus of Karelia National Park will find support. It has a unique ecosystem with world-wide significance and is worth restoring and preserving.

Sergei Tsvetkov
USSR 196191 Warshavskaja St. 45-III-41
Leningrad
Translated by W. Edward Nute

"The Integrity of Creation"
by Sister Betty Wolcott, OSF

Policy Statement Safeguarding the Health of the Earth and the Integrity of Creation, passed by Church Women United, New Orleans, Louisiana, USA, July 1989.

Prologue

We human beings have reached a point in our evolution where we have the power to decide whether the planet earth will live or die. More and more people are beginning to understand that the fate of the human race hangs in the balance with that of the earth, and that if life on the planet is to continue, we will need to change our ways of thinking and acting.

The problem isn't only the presence of the bomb, or the increasing population that could double in another forty years. Humans also have the potential to so violate the earth's processes as to cause the intricate set of biological, physical, and chemical interactions that make up the web of life , to fail and even to die. From the Industrial Revolution to the present time, humans, through their technology, have contaminated the waters, air, and soil with such reckless abandon that already in 1854 Chief Seattle warned: "Continue to contaminate your bed and you will one night suffocate in your own waste." Rain forests, so essential to the earth's equilibrium, and home to over half the earth's species, are being destroyed at the rate of a football field every 30 seconds. The irresponsible use of fossil fuels, other energy sources, and the use of plutonium, is not only depleting precious reserves, but jeopardizing the health of the earth's life support systems. Aquifers are being pimped dry; nuclear wastes are piling up and contaminating large areas. The protective ozone layer is under seige; raw sewage is washing up on the beaches; 100 species of plants and animals are becoming extince every single day; the food supply carries residues of toxic pesticides, and cancer cluster towns are springing up in many parts of the United States. These and many other symptoms tell us that something is dreadfully wrong.

Human beings, the late-comers on the planet earth, are causing the irreversible damage by drastically altering the earth's life support systems and interfering more and more in processes the earth has carried out for billions of years. These processed were always coded towards life. Time magazine, in its historic January 1, 1989, issue pointed out that the human race was at war with the planet. Since that war is threatening the very life of the earth, and ours, it is necessary to examine from a faith perspective why we are doing what we are doing in order that we may change our behavior and open the future to hope and healing.

Biblical Interpretation/Tradition

How we view our relationship to the earth and all the members of the community, and how we interpret God's intention for the earth, informs our responsibilities now and in the future. The Scriptures state that as the process of creation unfolded, God affirmed over and over that " . . . it was good." (Gn. 1) It is clear God was affirming the whole of the biological process that was emerging from the basic elements of the earth. Chief Seattle describes it thus: "We did not weave the web of life. We are merely a strand in it. Whatever we do to the web, we do it to ourselves." In the beginning, the planet earth was a beautiful, healthful, richly endowed home. The prophet Isiah reminds us "For thus says God, who created the heavens, who formed the earth and designed it . . . not to be waste, but to be lived in." (Is. 45:18-19)

The Scriptures portray the relationship between God and creation as covenantal and inclusive of God, humans, and earth. "This is a sign of the covenant which I make between me and you, and every living creature that is with you, for all future generations: I set my bow in the cloud, and it shall be a sign of the covenant between me and the earth." (Gn. 9:12-13) The earth was included in the covenant! Yahweh would entrust Israel with the gifts of land but there were expectations. They were to remember: "The land shall not be sold in perpetuity, for the land is mine; for you are strangers and sojourners with me." (Lev. 25:23) This implies no absolute control, personally or collectively, over the land.

In our times (when the terrible violence done to ceation--to nature and human beings-- is often fueled by an insatiable drive for domination, greed, and what is perceived as human progress), it is important to remember that keeping the Torah was a stipulation for holding land. The Israelites were not to have "golden calves"--other gods. They were to care for sisters and brothers, and to have special regard for widows and orphans; that is, for the most vulnerable in their midst. Today, the poor and powerless (people of color) are often forced to live in areas where pollution and toxic poisoning is the greatest. Renowned ecologist, Barry Commoner, states "There is a functional link between racism, poverty, and powerlessness, and the chemical industry's assault on the environment."

In Scripture the relationship between land and people is revealed to be so close that human behavior is reflected in the appearance of the land. "How long will the land mourn and the grass of the field wither? For the wickedness of those who dwell in it, the beasts and the birds are swept away." (Jer. 12:4) Noah, his family, and some animals were saved from the flood because Noah was a righteous person. Today the crimes against people and creation far exceed those in Noah's time. And while the rainbow in the sky may cause some to recall the Biblical story, the covenant is clearly ignored or forgotten, if it was every really understood.

In the New Testament, Jesus' teachings and life reveal important guidelines regarding our relationship to creation. The "greatest" are to serve, not dominate or exploit; the community is to be inclusive; and we can learn important lessons from the creation. "Look at the birds of the air . . . and consider the lilies of the field" and "unless the grain of wheat . . . dies it remains alone." (Mt. 6; John 12) (Finally our Franciscan tradition calls us to regard all creation as sisters and brothers, and to be of humble attitude, non-possessive, non-dominating, and all-inclusive.)

Alienation

The distancing of ourselves from the earth/land and the resulting ecological crises facing us are rooted in our origin stories--in those explanations of reality that have been handed down from generation to generation. How we view the earth's origins, and our own, underpins our belief systems, our cultures, socio-economic systems, our laws, healing systems- -everything. In Western Civilization, with its patriarchal underpinnings and infra-structures, the earth was viewed as apart from God and humans. It was as if escape from earth should be among the human's highest aspirations. While great importance was placed on the so-called spiritual and transcendent (since that was being closer to the Divine), the so-called material or temporal was denigrated, and given little importance. Eastern and Native peoples tended to see God present within the earth. The earth, then, was sacred and was not to be abused. No one had control over the earth; you could not own it. The breath of life, and power, and strength, and other qualities were believed to come to persons from connection to the earth community. It was through the earth that those gifts of the Spirit God were shared. From different world views, various opinions emerged about the earth, the Divine, and humankind. Many people are convinced that the mentality that spawned our ecological crisis comes from the Western interpretation with its dualistic and patriarchal-dominion-militaristic emphasis.

Women share with the earth this sense of alienation based on an erroneous but common interpretation of the Christian origin story. They have often been considered as unworthy of the highest human aspirations, as being more closely connected with earth and, therefore, farther away from the Divine.

The alienation of people from the earth is evident in both secular and religious areas of life. Only recently have church groups begun to include in their future plans and policy statements a concern for the earth and creation. For example, the World Council of Churches calls for "Justice, Peace, and the Integrity of Creation." The U.S. Catholic Bishops in their Pastoral Letter on Economics and Catholic Social Teaching include chapters on creation, but they are basically homo-centric, as are most church statements. Consider this statement in the Pastoral on Economics: " . . . every perspective on economic life that is human, moral, and Christian must be shaped by what the economy does for people and to people, and by how people participate in it." That same statement must be made on behalf of creation. Thus, every perspective on economic life that is human, moral, and Christian must be shaped by what the economy does for the earth, to the earth, and by how the earth participates in it. The statement in the pastoral letter reflects the stance that humankind lives apart from the earth rather than as intimate members who are one with the earth.

Beginnings/Origin Stories

We now know that the earth was not given to us ready made, but that it evolved over billions of years. Many people of faith believe that a Divine Source initiated the whole unfolding process of creation about 15 billion years ago with what physicists tell us was hydrogen. After about seven seconds, the hydrogen united and unfolded helium, and then carbon, and all the other elements emerged, and eventually life unfolded to such a degree of complexity that the earth could not only hear, see, and reproduce, (but) it could reflect on itself. In the human person the earth becomes conscious! Physicists now confirm that from the very beginning there have been vast inner, non-material dimensions to creation. Scientists can't explain those vast spiritual spaces of endless energy and activity--they can only tell us they are the same in every atom and that they have always been there. Those who believe that the Divine dwells in the earth interpret this inner dynamic force at the heart of the universe as the Spirit. The important fact that physicists affirm is that we are not different from the earth--we are the earth with soul. It is imperative that we accept that truth or we and the earth will not survive. Further, earth scientists and others tell us that at the heart of the creative process are laws or principles that guided and enabled the earth to evolve the complexity, diversity, and unique qualities, beauty, and abilities reflected in the earth's life community. These laws enabled the earth to be self-healing, self-governing, self-educating, and self-sustaining. If those laws or principles are reflections of the Creator's way of acting, we need to heed and obey them. We need to reshape our lives, our institutions and systems to reflect those principles.

Very briefly, the principles or laws are:
1. Differentiation: This is the dynamic within the evolutionary process that enabled the universe to emerge from . . . simplicity (hydrogen) to the complexity, out of which life awoke into consciousness. It is the principle that says it is good that you are differentiated from everything else. The ability and resilience of life to sustain and transit and transform itself is dependent on the diversity which supports it. Diversity is

essential to life. To wipe away our differences is to destroy truth, collective wisdom, and future life.

2. Interiority: Every part of creation has a unique identity, from atoms, to genes, to individual persons. Every member has integrity and truth. Each articulation of the universe is a unique expression of the whole and is truth; is a temple. The human can contemplate and reverence the sacred in each unique expression of creation.

3. Communion: From the very beginning, the universe has been in communion with itself in a spiritual and material way. There is an interdependent bonding of all of the parts of the universe, so much so that if the earth is sick, we will b sick. This bonding never violates the principles of differentiation or interiority, but rather enables them. In the human, this bonding is expressed also as love--love through conscious awareness and choice.

The new genesis stories or cosmologies tell us that not only are our own bodies temples of the Holy One, but that the created world which we so often disdain, oppress, and degrade in a myriad of ways is also the dwelling place of the Holy. We cannot be in communion with the earth in supporting life, healing, and transformation, without understanding the principles which guide the earth's life process, and without embracing our oneness with and dependence on that life process.

Today we are being called to choose life anew by "coming home" to who we really are. It is necessary to "come home" theologically and geographically--to become participating members of the life community of the earth where we live. The rationale for dealing with our ecological crises (in the way this policy statement attempts to do) is the firm conviction that we all are in some way polluters, subduers, and dominators. Not because we are evil, but because we are in need of deeper understandings of our connections to the Source and web of life. We, members of Church Women United, are being called upon to recommit ourselves to the covenant relationship with Yahweh, sisters and brothers, the earth, and the whole of creation. We covenant to respect and love differences, uniqueness, and community. Therefore, Church Women United, USA, calls its members:

1. To be inclusive of creation, incorporating the earth's wisdom and ways into everyday lives and activities.

2. To view ourselves as participating members of the community of life, not as its dominators.

3. To accept healing, inspiration, and support from the earth.

4. To use whenever possible only those products that the earth can recycle naturally.

5. To plant gardens, if only inflower pots, and share the experience with family and others.

6. To work legislatively for stronger laws to protect the water, air, and soil systems so that the earth may be restored to health.

7. To learn more about the laws of differentiation, interiority, and communion that guide the earth's unfolding of life, and integrate these principles into our work for justice and peace. To encourage and model conservation as well as responsible use of energy in all areas of life.

8. To work to protect all people, in particular the poor and those receiving the greatest impacts from the pollution and poisoning of the earth.

9. To spread the intent of this policy statement, and to write even better ones for our particular church and constituencies.

To order <u>A Collection of Voices</u>:

1 book: $11.95 (Californians, with sales tax: $12.79)
2-4 books: 20% off ($9.56 per book; Californians: $10.23 per book)
5-9 books, 30% off   ($8.36 and $8.95 respectively)
10-24 books, 40% off ($7.17 and $7.67)
25-49 books, 43% off ($6.81 and $7.29)
50-99 books, 46% off ($6.45 and $6.90)
100-199 books, 48% off ($6.21 and $6.64)
200 or more books, 50% off ($5.97 and $6.39)
(Prices include shipping.)

Please make your check payable to PK Publishing,
1420 College Avenue, Palo Alto, CA 94306 USA
(415) 856-4818, (415) 321-1994.
Allow 6-8 weeks delivery.

Thank you for helping to support Earth Day 1990